KALEIDOSCOPE KIDS

WHO *really* DISCOVERED AMERICA?

UNRAVELING THE MYSTERY & SOLVING THE PUZZLE

Avery Hart

Illustrations by
Michael Kline

WILLIAMSON PUBLISHING • CHARLOTTE, VT

DEDICATION

To Abbe Weiser, who has made wonderful discoveries and will make many more.

ACKNOWLEDGMENTS

Many thanks to Susan Williamson, Dana Pierson, Matthew Mantell, Elliot Raines, Victoria LaFortune, Ivan Van Sertima, Douglas Johnson, Steven MacWilliams, Irene Wagner, Joan Bracaglia, Ronn McGee, and the helpful people at Petroglyphs Park in Peterborough, Ontario, Canada.

Williamson's Kaleidoscope Kids® books
by Avery Hart and Paul Mantell:

PYRAMIDS!
50 Hands-On Activities to Experience Ancient Egypt

KNIGHTS & CASTLES
50 Hands-On Activities to Experience the Middle Ages

ANCIENT GREECE!
40 Hands-On Activities to Experience This Wonderous Age

Williamson's Kids Can!® books
by Avery Hart and Paul Mantell:

KIDS MAKE MUSIC!
Clapping & Tapping from Bach to Rock!

KIDS GARDEN!
The Anytime, Anyplace Guide to Sowing & Growing Fun

BOREDOM BUSTERS!
The Curious Kids' Activity Book

Library of Congress Cataloging-in-Publication Data

Hart, Avery.
   Who really discovered America? : unraveling the mystery & solving the puzzle/ by Avery Hart ; illustrations by Michael Kline.
      p. cm. – (A Kaleidoscope Kids book)
   Includes index.
   ISBN 1-885593-46-5(pbk.)
    1. America–Discovery and exploration–Study and teaching–Activity programs–Juvenile literature. [1.America–Discovery and exploration. 2. America–Historiography.] I. Kline, Michael P., ill. II. Title.

E101 .H34 200
970.01'076–dc21

                              00-043944

Kaleidoscope Kids® series editor: **Susan Williamson**
Interior design: **Marie Ferrante-Doyle**
Illustrations: **Michael Kline**
Cover design: **Black Fish Design**
Printing: **Quebecor World**

Photography: Tri-City Herald/Andre Ranieri, page 30; Petroglyphs Provincial Park, Ontario Parks, page 35; John Bingham/ Photo Researchers, Inc., page 37 (pyramid); Laurie Platt Winfrey, Inc., page 37 (Tenochtitlán); Mark C. Burnett/ Photo Researchers, Inc., page 38; Georg Gerster/ Photo Researchers, Inc., page 43; Dawn Ferreira, page 44; George Holton/ Photo Researchers, Inc., page 46; Andrew Rakoczy/ Photo Researchers, Inc., page 56; Laurie Platt Winfrey, Inc., page 59; George Holton/ Photo Researchers, Inc., page 60; Charles and Josette Lenars/CORBIS, page 65; Paul Daly/ nwpw.net, page 73; Acme Design Co., page 76.

Printed in Canada

Williamson Publishing Co.
P.O. Box 185
Charlotte, Vermont 05445
1-800-234-8791

10 9 8 7 6 5 4 3 2 1

CONTENTS

WHO REALLY DISCOVERED AMERICA?

The answer to that question is *so easy! Christopher Columbus* discovered America! It says so in history books. Our parents and teachers have told us. We have seen it on TV, and in the movies, too. We even celebrate a holiday for him!

Everybody knows that Columbus sailed to America in 1492. He found some natives living there. Then, he claimed the land for Spain, and America was discovered.

End of story.

But is it, really?

After all, the lands of America — with millions of people living on them — were already there before he came. Columbus may have "found" America, but in fact, it never was lost! For untold ages, American lands have been home to many people, with different ways of looking at life and different styles of living.

The discovery of America is like a puzzle with some pieces as big as a mountain and others as tiny as a scrap. But it's a puzzle worth solving. When we put pieces from America's long neglected past together, we discover the heritage of all Americans, past, present, and future.

As you read these words, you are about to enter a world of discovery. It's *as if* you are standing on a mountain, in front of a cave. You want to go in deeper and get a look around. Searching for

America's roots will take you to many places — mountains, deserts, fields, coastlines, universities, and even cyberspace!

To explore, you have to travel light, by letting go of any opinions you may have about ancient America. Old ideas are too heavy to bring on a discovery journey. But luckily, brains and creativity are easy to carry. You'll need them, for sure!

As for other equipment, remember to bring a light, a pickax, and a writing tool and notebook.

The best light is a bright mind, one that is open and ready to track down the truth.

The pickax will help chip away false ideas and move age-old myths out of the way as you uncover new territory.

As for the writing tool and notebook, they stand for what *you* make of your discoveries, activities, crafts, creations, and the conclusions you come to. Just think — your expanded thoughts about the discovery of America will actually add to the world's understanding, because *you* are an important part of this world!

There's the mountain ahead of you, Truth Tracker, with the Cave of the Ancient Past wide open. Are you ready to move into the mystery of America's history? Then, step right in by turning the page!

WHAT HAVE YOU DISCOVERED LATELY?

What does it mean to "discover" something? Does it mean finding something, as in discovering dinosaur bones in your backyard? Or does it mean learning, as in discovering the answer to a math puzzle?

Does discovery have to include risk-taking or hard work, as in a trip to the South Pole to study the life cycle of penguins? Or is it about being the first one to see something, as in discovering water on Mars?

Oh, yes, there's a lot to discover about discoveries!

QUICK! DEFINE DISCOVERY!

Human beings — meaning *you* and everyone you know — are walking, talking discovery machines.

You have probably discovered lots of things lately. Maybe it was a new kind of music or food. Maybe you found out that a kid at school shares your interests. Maybe you learned that your mom was once a majorette or that you enjoy photography.

Before we move into the mystery of America's history, think about what discovery means. The more you explore what discovery might be, the more your ideas about who really discovered America will grow. Discovery has a way of making that happen!

Think about it!

"One Small Step for Man . . . One Giant Leap for Mankind"

Who *discovered* the moon? Did the first people to see the moon discover it? Or did Neil Armstrong discover it when he landed on the moon? And does that mean the United States owns the moon?

Great "Discoveries" — Or Were They Really?

Here are some famous "discoveries." Each one is unique, meaning one of a kind. Does one of them seem like it is *not* a true discovery?

? Did Pocahontas *discover* England? (She was one of the first Native Americans to visit there.)

? Did Benjamin Franklin *discover* electricity? (He experimented with lightning.)

? Did Einstein *discover* the Theory of Relativity? (He explained a law of nature that no one had thought of before.)

? Did Jonas Salk *discover* the oral polio vaccine? (He found out how to prevent a disease.)

? Did the Wright brothers *discover* the airplane? (They invented the flying machine.)

? Did George Washington Carver *discover* peanut butter? (He experimented with peanuts in his laboratory.)

Try It!

Think of three discoveries you have made in the past year. Your list will be proof that you live in a world of discovery!

Who Really Discovered America?

Was it . . .

. . . the first people to *see* America?

. . . the first people to *wander* on American soil?

. . . the first people to *settle* in America?

. . . the first people to *bring news* of America back to others?

. . . the first people to *trade goods* with people in America?

. . . the first people to own American land *legally?*

Different experts have different answers to these questions. But fortunately, *everyone* agrees on a couple of facts about America.

WHERE ARE THE AMERICAS?

*F*act #1:

The Americas are located in the *Western Hemisphere*, on the opposite side of the world from the Eastern Hemisphere, where Europe, Africa, Asia, and Australia are located. ("Hemisphere" means half a sphere.)

We call the two "sides" of the world Eastern and Western because of tradition and because naming them helps keep things clear. In reality, of course, it's all one world, and being round, it doesn't have sides at all!

WHO IS AN AMERICAN?

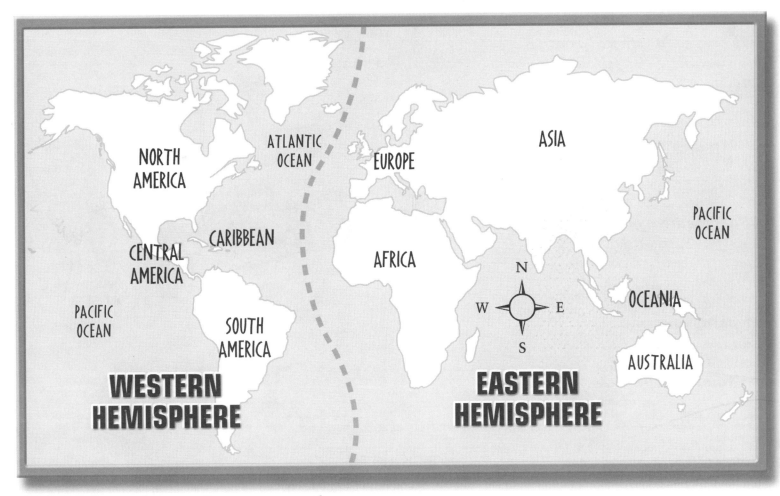

See how the continents relate to one another.

*F*_{act #2:}

If you live in the United States of America, you call yourself an American. To you, the name "America" stands for your homeland, the good old U.S.A. But did you know that there are other Americas and other Americans, too?

Canadians, for example, are Americans since they live in North America. Mexicans, Central Americans, South Americans, and the islanders of the Caribbean Sea are all Americans, too.

All people who live in the Western Hemisphere have the right to call themselves Americans.

A WESTERN HEMISPHERE E-PAL

Wouldn't it be great if the people of the Western Hemisphere could all be friends? Well, how about getting the process started by communicating with a fellow, but foreign, American?

You can write to a fellow American from an English-speaking American nation. Or, if you are learning French, Spanish, or Portuguese, communicating with a native speaker is great practice. And kids who speak French and Spanish are often eager to practice their English, too.

American English-speaking countries: Parts of Canada, the United States, Belize, Guyana

American French-speaking countries: Parts of Canada, Haiti, French Guinea, and the French West Indies (Martinique, Guadeloupe, St. Barthélemy, St. Martin).

American Portuguese-speaking countries: Brazil

American Spanish-speaking countries: All the rest!

–French–
J'ai volé au Canada.
(I flew to Canada.)

–Spanish–
Mi hogar está en Méjico.
(My home is in Mexico.)

–English–
I have friends in Brazil!

–Portuguese–
Meu irmão vive em Minnesota.
(My brother lives in Minnesota.)

To find an e-pal, go to <**www.About.com**> and click on Kids in the main menu. Then, on the Kids' page, click on Pen Pals for Kids. Be sure to ask your pal who really discovered America. You might be surprised by the answer!

Home, Sweet Hemisphere!

Globes and atlases (books of maps) are basic tools for discovering places on planet Earth. (If you don't have one or the other at home, try a website like <**www.nationalgeo graphic.com**> or a library.)

Look at the Western Hemisphere, home of the Americas (see page 9). What do you notice about it? Is South America located *directly* under North America?

Where are America and Asia closest? How about Africa and America, and Europe and America? Where is the hemisphere widest?

If you were to have traveled from one place to another during ancient times, what route would you have taken? What continent seems closest to the Americas? (Tuck your hemisphere observations away for future reference in your sleuthing.)

Words — And What They Mean to You!

Here are the 13 definitions of "discover" that we found in our dictionary:

*"Discover:
to see,
get knowledge of,
find,
find out,
learn about,
gain sight or knowledge of
something that had existed
but was unknown or unfound,
detect (catch in the act, or find
out truth about),
espy (to see in the distance),
descry (to make out something
in the distance by looking
carefully),
unearth,
ferret out,
notice,
devise a new use for something
already known."*

That's a pretty big definition. But then, discovery is a pretty big idea!

PRINT THE WESTERN HEMISPHERE

Find the biggest potato in the world (well, a big one, anyway) and cut it in half the long way. One half will be North America and the other South America. Use a sharp knife to outline the basic shape of each continent on the potato halves (you may first want to trace them on a piece of paper).

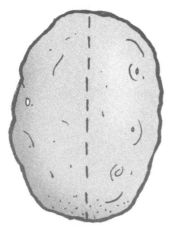  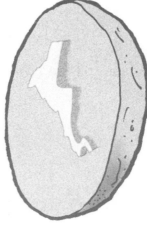

1 *Put the northern half of Central America at the bottom of the "north" potato. Put the southern part of Central America at the top of the "south" potato.*

2 *Whittle around the outline with a plastic knife. (Don't forget Cuba and other Caribbean islands.)*

3 *Dip the potato lightly in paint to make stamps. (If you have a snail-mail pal, use light-colored paint to make cool stationery.)*

A Quick Course in Historical Sleuthing . . .
Or, How to Find the Truth!

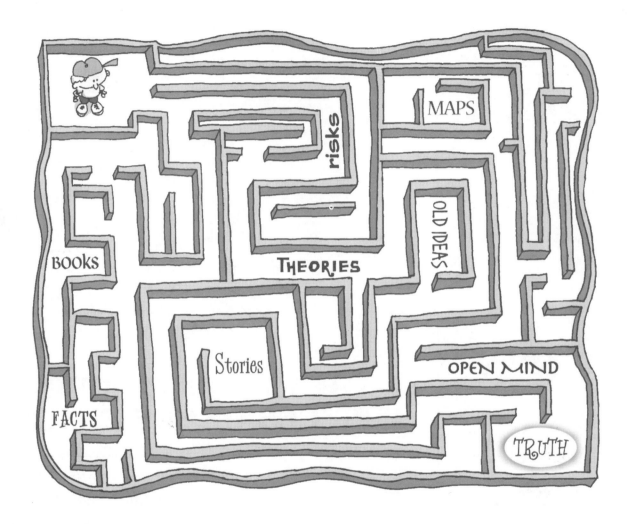

Well, Truth Tracker, how can we possibly discover the truth about the past? After all, we weren't there, so we cannot be eyewitnesses. And every passing day brings us further from the actual events.

Until someone invents a time machine, we can't travel back in time. (Hope you're working on it!) Discovering the past will take some doing. And the "doing" part begins with hunting for clues.

CLUES: THEY'RE EVERYWHERE!

A piece of metal stuck in the earth, the charcoal remains of a fire, certain words or legends, a particular custom, a rock with a chip on the edge — all can be clues to the past. Even that funny feeling, the one we call a "hunch" can be a clue. But it's going to take more than clues to explore America's past; we'll need facts and theories, too.

FACTS AND THEORIES: PIECES OF THE PUZZLE

The discovery of America is like a 500-piece puzzle without a box top showing the finished, "put-together" puzzle. There are lots of little pieces with bits of color and patterns. By matching pieces, you can build a section that fits in *somewhere*. And as you try fitting different pieces together, you wonder what the whole picture might be, taking clues from the actual pieces themselves.

Facts are like the actual puzzle pieces that you can hold. *Theories* are ideas and explanations that you come up with after you think about the facts.

The Truth, with a Capital "T"

Albert Einstein

*I*t's time to put on a thinking cap (even if it's an old baseball cap.) You need brainpower for this theory about theories!

The Total Truth Theory

It is *impossible* to discover the total truth about *anything*, because the complete and total truth is always slightly out of reach. In other words, life is bigger and more amazing than *anyone's* ideas about it.

Finding "The Total Truth" is more like the game of being "hot" (close to something) or "cold" (far from it). Theories can only bring us closer or further from truth; they cannot bring us face-to-face with the absolute truth.

Albert Einstein, the great scientific genius, believed this theory. At the end of his long life of discovery, he wrote that life was a wonderful mystery and always would be!

The Search for Truth

Are you wondering, "If the truth is out of reach, why bother looking for it?" It's a good question. Our answer is that it *feels* better to ask questions and discover answers that bring us *closer* to the truth. We think life has more sparkle when there's always another layer to discover! Would you be bored if you instantly knew the "whole truth" about everything?

JOIN THE SEARCH!

To explore America's past, you don't have to be a trained researcher, historian, or teacher. Ordinary people like you and me have made amazing discoveries about history. Still, it's cool to realize that a whole army of diggers, explorers, professors, investigators, researchers, and assorted scientists are busy working — all eager to solve the puzzle of America's history, too.

The "army" includes *archaeologists*, who study the ancient past; *paleontologists*, who focus on what fossils and bones can tell us; *anthropologists*, who study how people live; *linguists*, who study languages; and *sociologists*, who study societies and cultures. They have developed tools and techniques to uncover the past — tools and techniques that you can borrow.

Tool #1: Artifacts — Keys to the Past

Experts call any objects made or used by humans *artifacts*. Artifacts can be as big as a car or as tiny as a speck of powder. They are crucial bits of evidence that open up paths of thinking because someone, sometime, left each artifact behind. Artifacts are usually found deep in the ground. That's because planet Earth is very gradually being covered with new soil, debris, and other kinds of "dust." Over thousands of years, it all adds up — and covers up! That's why ancient artifacts are found usually by digging, digging, and digging some more.

MEET THE PAST . . . IN YOUR ROOM

Artifacts of our time are everywhere, right out in the open! They're practically looking at you, waiting for discovery. What are the oldest artifacts in your environment (home, yard, or school)? Look carefully. These items will not jump up and say, "Hello." You have to search them out.

1 *Survey the area.* Slow down and notice what's around. Then, pick out a few artifacts to investigate. Think about the **who, what, when, where, why,** and **how** of each artifact.

2 *Look for clues.* Is it decorative or useful, or both? Where might it have been before it was brought here? What does it reveal about the person or people who used it? (These items can reveal a lot!)

3 *Ask questions.* How old is each artifact? If you don't know exactly, how can you find out? Is there someone who would know? Does the item reveal a secret about the past? For example, suppose your great-grandfather was in a war that he never spoke about. Maybe he wrote a letter back then that your family still has. What a discovery that artifact would be! Or, maybe your grandmother has an old recipe from the country where her parents were born. Prepare the recipe as a tasty link to your family's past.

4 *Look for more links.* Ask as many questions as you can to find other links to the past or your family history. Let each answer lead you to another question! It's fun — especially if you like detective work!

More Artifacts — Hunt for Oop-Art

What in the world is an *oop-art*? It's an archaeological term for *out-of-place ARTifact* — an artifact that was made in one place, but was found in another.

Oop-art is exciting because it shows how people moved and interacted. In the search for who really discovered America, this is critical information. For example, artwork thought to have been created by the Olmec of Mexico has been found in the buildings of Chaco Canyon, New Mexico, in North America. The art could be proof that the native people of North and South America had early contact with each other, despite the great distance separating them.

Try It !

What oop-art is in your home or school? How did it get there? What questions does it raise? Use oop-art to discover who lived in your house or apartment before you, or where your ancestors lived.

Tool #2: Wood Dating

Wood dating, called *dendrochronology*, measures the age of wooden products. The word is from Greek: *dendro*, meaning wood, and *chronology*, meaning the study of time.

Here's how it works: Each season a tree grows a ring around its inner core. If the tree has gotten enough water and light, the ring is thicker than it would be if conditions had been harsh.

By comparing ring patterns and using computer models, we can date any kind of wood — old house beams, tool handles, or tent stakes. Dendrochronology has dated objects that are 8,000 years old!

ESTIMATING A TREE'S AGE

How old is that tree in your yard or the park — the big one? Be a modern dendrochronologist and find out (without cutting it down, of course!).

You don't have to be a math wizard to do this. The basic formula is easy: $D \times SM = A^*$

"D" is the **diameter** *(width) of the tree, in inches. "SM" is the* **species multiplier,** *a special number for each tree species (see chart below).*

When you multiply them, you get "A," the tree's **approximate age.**

1 *Measure a tree from a species listed below. First, find a point on the tree's trunk that is 4½ feet (135 cm) from the ground. At that spot, find the tree's approximate diameter by having a friend hold a yardstick straight across the trunk. Write down the diameter in inches. **

2 *Then, multiply the diameter by the multiplier to come up with the tree's approximate age.*

Species	Multiplier
Silver Maple, Poplar, Elm	2
Sycamore, Pin Oak, Red Oak, Honey Locust	3.5
Birch, Sugar Maple, Black Cherry, Norway Spruce	4
White Oak, Laurel Oak, White Ash	5
Chestnut, Hickory	7

3 *Check your tree's age estimate with someone who knows the history of the tree. How close did you come?*

*This formula works only when the diameter is measured in inches, not centimeters.

Tool #3: Carbon Dating

No, we don't mean going to the movies! In archaeology, *dating* means discovering the age of an object. Carbon is one of the most common elements on earth. Some of it — just a miniscule (very tiny) amount — is radioactive. As the radioactive carbon decays, it turns into regular carbon at a very precise rate. By measuring just how much has decayed, scientists can figure out the age of bones and other *organic* matter (material that has carbon in it), almost exactly. With carbon dating, scientists can date archaeological finds as far back as 60,000 years!

Tool #4: Languages Wanted — Dead or Alive!

Languages can be "living," meaning still spoken, or "dead," no longer used. Both reveal important clues to the past.

For example, have you said the word "Hi" recently? Did you know you were speaking Icelandic? Now, how did an Icelandic word get on *your* lips?

Or, maybe you've gone "berserk" a few times in your life (not too often, we hope!) Berserk is from Old Norse, spoken by the Vikings. (A big clue to how it got here is on pages 36 and 64.)

We guess words like *hi, berserk,* and others can be called *oop-words — out-of-place words*. Like some of America's discoverers, these oop-words made themselves right at home!

Learn the Lingo: "Field Trips," "Sites," and "Finds"

Sometimes, to discover the past, you've got to be on the go! A "field trip" is the actual visit. (You've probably been on a few!) A "site" is any place you go to gain information. And a "find" is the information or artifacts you discover there.

about it!

Gezundheit! Salsa! Bon Voyage!

Foreign words color languages and intermix around the world. Listen for them in school and at home. Count how many you hear (many of them are not obvious because we get used to hearing them). Then, see if you can discover how those words ended up in your world.

Tool #5: Hunches and Intuition

Many a discovery has come from somebody's *intuition* (in-too-IH-shun), which is a kind of "knowing" that comes from the dreamy side of the brain. People who believe in intuition say it feels like a hunch or a thought coming "out of the blue." Some hunches are strong; you feel you know the truth about something.

TRACKING EVIDENCE

Tracking evidence means letting one piece of information lead you to the next. When you track evidence, you follow "leads" and ferret out facts, piece by piece, as you try to prove or disprove something. Hunches can help you decide which leads to follow and which to ignore.

But be careful, Truth Tracker: Evidence and proof can be slippery stuff. Remember, there is always another layer to discover and another way to think!

Try It!

Ask your friends and family if they've ever experienced a strong hunch or intuition and, if so, what it was like. You will probably hear some interesting stories!

THINK about it!

It's *Obvious:* The Earth is Flat!

Life is funny. Sometimes, you can't believe what you see!

Imagine standing outside with a friend who says, "The earth is flat and I can prove it!"

"Okay," you might say. "What's your evidence?"

The other kid gives you a look that says, "Duh! Just look around you. It's *obvious* that the earth is flat!"

What *obvious* ideas of today do you think might someday be proven to be false?

Internet Discovery: Check the Sites

The Internet has "sites" where you can make "finds," too. Check out Web Weaver's North America Archaeology Links at <**www.mtsu.edu/~gdennis/**> to discover a possible field trip. The site lists ancient places in the United States, and one may be near you!

Five-Point "Star Guide"

Truth tracking is not easy — tools or no tools! How can you know if an idea is closer to or further from the truth? Try using our *Five-Point Star Guide* to weigh the merits of ideas you come across.

Draw a five-fingered star; the whole star represents one theory. Each finger on the star is worth 0 to 5 points, 5 being the most that any finger can earn. As you proceed through the book, indicate the points you award each theory, the highest being 25 for a theory that you believe is absolutely true. Later (at the end of the book), compare your results to rate the theories.

Point 1. **Start with what you know** *(use it as a "home base" if an idea becomes confusing). Does the new theory support the facts as you know them? (0 to 5 points)*

Point 2. **Throw out old opinions.** *Ask yourself: Is my mind really open? Or do I secretly want a particular idea to be true (or untrue)? (0 to 5 points)*

Point 3. **Review the theory evidence.** *What specific evidence supports this theory, and how reliable is it? (0 to 5 points)*

Point 4. **Use intuition.** *What does your gut say about the theory? (This is different from wanting it to be true. In fact, often what you want to be true and what your intuition tells you don't agree.) (0 to 5 points)*

Point 5. **Put it all together.** *Overall, does the idea make sense and fit with the other puzzle pieces? (0 to 5 points)*

There's no shame in changing your mind. That just shows you are an open-minded detective, evaluating new evidence as it comes to you!

A TEST CASE

Okay, Truth-Tracker, let's test your detective skills by examining the evidence of one of the most widely believed theories of who really discovered America. The best way, we think, to approach these theories is to read them first – with an open mind. Gauge your "gut" reaction. Then read the evidence "for" and "against." You'll find oftentimes that there is a convincing argument both for and against the same theory. Evaluate according to the *Five-Point Star Guide* and see where the theory stands – for now at least. As you learn more and make your own discoveries, you may wish to revise your evaluation. That makes you an excellent detective – one who is always open to new ideas! So, here we go!

THE LAND-BRIDGE THEORY ＊ ＊ ＊ ＊ ＊ ＊ ＊ ＊ ＊ ＊ ＊ ＊ ＊ ＊

About 18,000 years ago, during an ice age, planet Earth was like a ball of ice cream. Glaciers – up to two miles high – covered North America and dripped down South America.

But between Russia in Asia and Alaska in North America was a strip of land without water. And no water means no ice. This strip became a kind of "land bridge" connecting Asia and North America.

Large animals – wooly mammoths, bison, and mastodons – used the bridge; people followed, hunting and gathering food.

As the ice melted, the people and their ancestors continued wandering southward for thousands of years. Some stopped and settled along the way, becoming farmers rather than living as nomadic hunters and gatherers. Others continued south, and little by little, America was discovered.

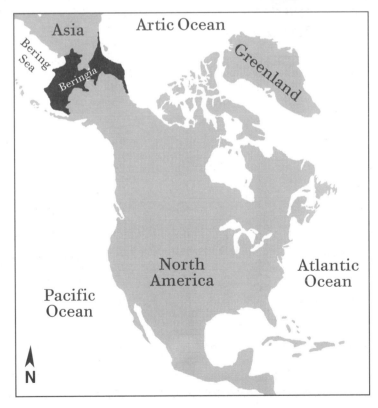

Land bridge at Beringia where the Bering Strait is today.

EVIDENCE *FOR* THE LAND-BRIDGE THEORY

• It's a fact that a land bridge between Asia and America really existed in the ancient past. The two continents were connected at a place called Beringia, where the Bering Strait is today.

• It's also a fact that many Native Americans share similar physical features with Asians. According to the Land-Bridge Theory, that is because their long-lost ancestors actually were Asians.

• It's **obvious** to many that prehistoric people could not make ships strong enough to travel from continent to continent. (Note that this is an opinion.)

• Even though not a single artifact has been found to support the Land-Bridge Theory, some will be found someday! (It's hard looking for artifacts under a frigid sea!) So, not having artifacts doesn't mean that there aren't any.

EVIDENCE *AGAINST* THE LAND-BRIDGE THEORY

• One professor who studies ancient languages believes that the first American languages started in Mexico and moved north on the lips of wandering people. How could languages move north if people were heading south, as the Land-Bridge Theory suggests?

• In the 1970s, the body of a super-ancient ice age woman was found in Asia, a land mass home to dark-haired people. But this ancient human was a redhead! How, then, had she gotten there? Experts realized that they did not really understand how people had spread out on the earth many thousands of years ago.

• In the 1960s, experts found proof that ancient people **had sailed** to Australia. That means that ancients might have built ships and also reached the Americas by sea.

• Despite a lot of looking for many years, not one single artifact has been found to support the theory.

Take the "Star Guide" Challenge!

Hmmm! See how this works? If you don't have a completely open mind, the same evidence can be used for *and* against a theory. Before you read more, use the *Star Guide* on page 22.

Does *your* personal conclusion about the Land-Bridge Theory agree with your *Star Guide* number? (If you think it is very likely to be true, you will have a number close to 25.)

THE THEORY THAT LOST ITS LUSTER ★ ★ ★ ★ ★ ★ ★ ★ ★

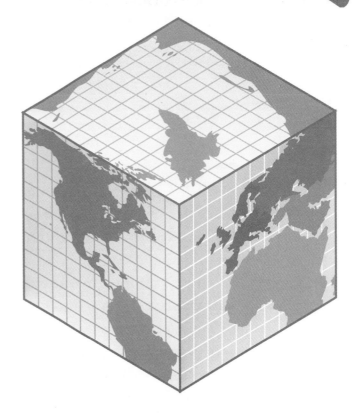

You can still find historians and books that treat the Land-Bridge Theory as if it were the *one and only truth* about America's discovery. But new books (like this one!) have been written because most experts now agree that the Land-Bridge Theory is not true — not the *who*, not the *where*, not the *how*, not the *why*, and certainly not the *when*.

Yes, Asians *did* trek to America over a land bridge — which is a kind of discovery in itself. But they probably came about 7,000 years *after* others had already arrived! (See how parts of a theory can be true, but the conclusion is not accurate because part of the truth was out of our "sight"?)

Einstein was right: Life is a mystery! The land bridge is *part* of the puzzle of America's discovery, but not the whole picture.

The search continues!

PREHISTORY & THE ANCIENTS

People were here, all right, long before Europeans arrived. Tracking down the very first Americans takes some doing, but remember that army of searchers and diggers out there has found a few clues and artifacts we can examine, even if time is not on our side.

There's a footprint, some old bones, rock art, and copper mines. So turn on your light and get your pickax ready.

The questions are: Who were these ancient Americans — and who were their ancestors? Who got here first? And for us, the big question is: How do we Truth Trackers evaluate the proof, the facts, the clues, and the evidence so we know which theory or theories to believe? Your handy *Star Guide* will get a workout here!

THE OLDEST CLUE: A FOOTPRINT

Have you ever left footprints as you walked along the shore? The ocean probably washed them away soon after. But once — about 13,000 years ago — another child left a footprint, deep in a peat bog. Talk about a lasting impression!

The print was found in Monte Verde, Chile, in South America. Near it were stone tools, the remains of huts, tent stakes, the bones of butchered birds and camels, and carved ivory artifacts. Also nearby was a shallow hole in the ground, full of nutshells, fruit pits, and charcoal.

FERRET OUT FACTS

History is more than dates and facts. Good historians bring history to life by ferreting out the facts and putting those puzzle pieces together for a partial picture.

1 *Use the information to pick out **facts** about the child from Monte Verde.*

2 *From the finds at the site, what do you imagine the child did for food, water, and shelter, and for companionship?*

3 *Write a story or rap about the child of Monte Verde and bring history to life.*

HUMAN CLUES:
REMAINS OF ANCIENT AMERICANS

The people who lived 8, 9, or 10 *thousand* years ago are long gone. But some of their bones, teeth, bodies, clothes, and shoes still remain! So far, the remains of about 12 ancient individuals have been found in the Americas.

Since their true names are lost in time, scientists have given them new ones (usually associated with where they were found or who found them) such as *Spirit Caveman, Kennewick Man,* and *Arlington Springs Woman.* The remains are excellent clues to the past, but in the puzzling world of ancient America, they sometimes raise more questions than they answer!

MAKE YOUR OWN FOOTPRINT

You, too, can make a lasting impression! You'll need a shoebox lid and some plaster of paris.

1 *Mix 2 cups (500 ml) of plaster using the directions on the box.*

2 *Spray the inside of the lid with cooking oil. Clean and spray the bottom of your foot (or hand), too.*

3 *When the plaster is soupy, pour it into the lid.**

4 *Wait a couple of minutes (not too long) and gently put your foot (or hand) in the plaster to make an impression.*

5 *Scratch your name and age next to it. Who knows? Somebody may hang your print in a museum 13,000 years from now!*

*Note: Please don't pour any leftover plaster down the toilet or the sink drain. (It will clog your pipes when it hardens!) Just pour it into the trash.

BRINGING HISTORY TO LIFE:

SPIRIT CAVEMAN'S LAST DAY

Surrounded by cattails and grass, the man sat by a lake. His head probably hurt in two places. The fracture in his skull was healing, but the sores in his gums were not.

He caught some fish in a net, boiled them, and ate them. Then, he laid down for his final rest. The infection in his mouth had spread, and he quietly passed away.

Others found him and wrapped him in a robe of rabbit fur and hemp. They dug a shallow grave, lined it with reeds, and laid him in it. Beside him, they placed his prized moccasins, the ones that had been patched twice with antelope hide.

About 9,400 years later, anthropologists would discover him and name him Spirit Caveman.

Think About It:
Our Ideas about Prehistoric People

When you think "Stone Age," do you see ape-like humans carrying clubs, acting like the Flintstones? Those ideas may be fun, but they are way off the mark!

Take Spirit Caveman, for instance. His robe was woven from plants and fur. His net and moccasins were well made, too. The people who found him treated him gently and respectfully.

What do you know now about Spirit Caveman that surprises you?

Tom McClelland of Richland, WA, shows the skull casting of Kennewick Man he and anthropologist Jim Chatters used to recreate the facial features of the 9,200-year-old discovery.

Think About It: # You Be The Judge

If you were the judge or jury deciding the outcome of the Kennewick Man case, who would you give his remains to? The scientists? The Native Americans? Or the Viking descendants?

Can you think of a way to compromise and satisfy all the parties?

Meet Kennewick Man: A Modern Celebrity!

An 8,000-year-old celeb? You bet! Kennewick Man, who was found in the state of Washington in the United States, has been in the news lots of times! His first splash of fame came when one expert suggested he was European. That was big news because there is no other solid proof that Europeans had been in the Western Hemisphere so long ago.

Then, *another* expert disagreed with the first and suggested that Kennewick Man was Polynesian, from islands in the Pacific. That was big news because it proved that people had traveled to America over water.

When we were writing this book, Kennewick Man was the focus of a three-way lawsuit.

◈ Scientists wanted his remains in order to study them.

◈ Native Americans wanted to "give him back to Mother Earth" by burying him according to their traditions.

◈ A third group claimed he was a long lost Viking, deserving of a Scandinavian-style burial.

We wonder if Kennewick Man ever dreamed he'd be so famous!

Friendly vs. Unfriendly Disagreements

Conflicting ideas about the first Americans have led to many debates and arguments among archaeologists as they share information. Fortunately, the "experts" usually argue in a friendly way. After all, it's normal and natural for people to disagree; it's *how* we do it that matters.

Friendly Disagreements	*vs.*	*Unfriendly Disagreements*
• People use friendly language.		• People say mean, insulting things.
• People can "agree to disagree."		• People try to force each other into admitting they are wrong.
• Communication improves because people share different points of view.		• Because people don't listen to other points of view, communication shuts down.
• They feel okay — and often are stimulating and fun.		• They feel yucky.
• They leave room for people to change their minds and come up with completely new ideas.		• They keep people stuck in their opinions with closed minds.

Make sure that your next disagreement, argument, or discussion is friendly. Show respect to the other person by listening to his or her ideas, even if you don't agree with them.

A MULTICULTURAL PAST?

Different Races

It's a mystery: The remains of the American ancients are not all alike! Some have wide faces and some, narrow ones. Some have slanted eyes and others, round ones. Some are unlike anyone of today, but still distinctly human. Scientists don't understand the mix of faces, features, skin, and hair. But some say it matches a theory of *multiple migration* ("multiple" means many; "migration" means moving from one place to another).

THE MULTIPLE-MIGRATION THEORY ✳ ✳

This theory says that the first people to discover the Western Hemisphere came by boats, in small groups, over a period of thousands of years. They came from many different places. Once here, they interacted, sometimes fighting and sometimes marrying each other. Some experts believe that the original arrivals died out when new arrivals attacked them.

Does the Multiple-Migration Theory sound like modern America to you, with all kinds of people, sometimes struggling to get along?

Maybe part of the struggle comes from the belief that human beings come in different races: Light-skinned people are part of the Caucasian race, dark-skinned people are in the Negro race, and people with yellow skin color and dark, narrow eyes belong to the Asian race.

But is humanity really divided into different races?

Let's take a closer look.

Scientists have proven that all human beings are made of the same basic material: blood, bone, skin, hair, etc. They say that we are chemically and biologically *more than* 99 percent alike and *less* than one percent different. That means that the darkest person, the lightest person, and everyone in between, are made of *the same stuff!*

Because of this, scientists gave up the idea of separate races about 40 years ago. So, pass it on: *The only race that actually exists is the human race!*

KING WODEN-LITHI
DISCOVERED AMERICA 4,000 YEARS AGO!

What's that? You've *never heard* of King Woden-lithi? Well, neither have most people! But Dr. Barry Fell of Harvard University wrote about the ancient Scandinavian king and the trip he made to America long, long ago.

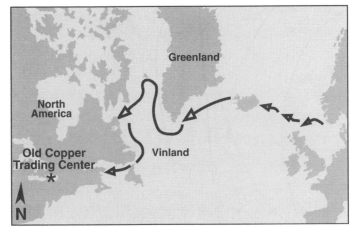

Woden-lithi's route across the Atlantic and up the St. Lawrence River in North America.

An artist's rendition of how King Woden-lithi may have appeared.

THE WODEN-LITHI THEORY ★ ★ ★ ★ ★ ★ ★ ★ ★ ★ ★ ★ ★ ★

Woden-lithi, whose name means "the king who serves the god Woden," lived in the land we now call Norway, one of the Scandinavian countries. Sailing across the Atlantic Ocean, Woden-lithi went up the St. Lawrence River in about 1750 B.C. There, in the place we now call Toronto, Canada, he created a trading center.

Woden-lithi and his crew exchanged hand-woven cloth for lumps of pure copper. The copper was provided by the world's first known metal workers, who were part of the Old Copper culture of the Great Lakes region.

The king made no claim of ownership of North America. He and the natives seemed to trust each other in business and may have even worshiped together. After visiting from April to September, Woden-lithi returned home to Norway. But he left clear instructions for the crew that was staying behind to continue his center. Those instructions were written in rock and can still be seen today!

EVIDENCE *FOR* THE WODEN-LITHI THEORY * *

• Rock art and writing, called *petroglyphs*, were discovered in Canada in 1954. Included with Algonquin Indian art made over the ages is a picture of a boat with a Norse-style masthead. How could American natives have pictured such a ship without ever seeing one?

• The rock art also includes pictures of the Norse sun god, the hammer of Thor, and the spear of Woden, plus writing in *Ogam* (AH-gum) and *Cosaine* (CO-sain), two ancient languages. The art has been dated to 3000 to 400 B.C., the same time that Dr. Fell (see page 33) believes Woden-lithi visited America.

• Experts have found similar petroglyphs in Scandinavia, the Caribbean, and even Arabia! To Dr. Fell and some others, this is proof that explorers at this time traveled far and wide across oceans and land.

EVIDENCE *AGAINST* THE WODEN-LITHI THEORY

• Many people who doubt Dr. Fell's ideas say that the rock carvings may just be random markings on stone, with no real meaning.

• Others say that natives made the symbols, which have nothing to do with King Woden-lithi or any other Europeans.

Accidentally on Purpose?

Do you think King Woden-lithi arrived in North America by accident or on purpose? If you think it was by accident, then why did he arrive with goods to trade? If you think it was on purpose, how did he know America was there?

WHAT DO YOU SEE?

Imagine that you are an archaeologist who has to make sense of these Canadian petroglyphs.

1 *What do you see in the shapes?*

2 *What do you think is being communicated?*

3 *Compare your impressions with the impressions of others.*

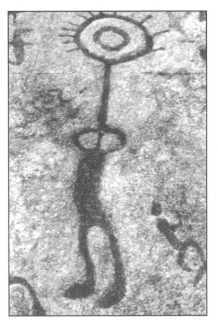

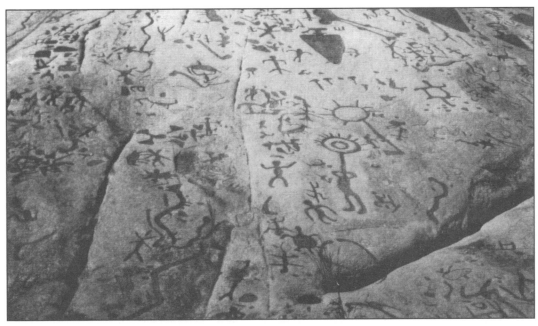

Hundreds of petroglyphs on a flat expanse of marble at Petroglyphs Provincial Park in Canada. It is believed that the figures were carved between 600 and 1,000 years ago.

Close-up of carving thought to be of Gitchi Manitou, the Great Spirit and creator of the world, according to some Native Americans. The sun is said to be its home.

Is It Wednesday?

If it is, it's Woden's Day (say it fast), which is the original meaning of the word "Wednesday." Woden was the Norse* god of power. We use the names of other Norse gods and goddesses in English, too. *Thursday* comes from *Thor's Day* for the Norse god of thunder. *Friday* is *Freya's Day* for the goddess of strength and peace. (See the explanation on page 20 for oop-words.)

Experts believe that Norse spiritual beliefs were similar to Native American beliefs.

*Have you noticed something? So far, we've used three words to refer to the Scandinavian region and its people: Viking, Norse, and Scandinavian.

HOW SIMILAR ARE OUR IDEAS, ANYWAY?

Remember how we said that all people share 99 percent of the same "stuff"? Well, what if we all shared a large percent of the same emotional responses to things and the same thought processes, too? Then, petroglyphs — with similar images — or similar tools, or similar beliefs, might prove that all humanity shares more than just biology and chemistry. And it might prove that theories based on worldwide similarities (in, for example, the design of a mast) don't mean that people traveled and shared ideas at all. They just all think alike! Now, that could be a theory to wipe out all the other theories! What do you think?

1 *Do an experiment to see how closely (or not) we all think. Give five people the same scenario, the same time limit, and the same supplies.*

2 *Tell each person to imagine he is lost on a mountain, it looks like rain, and it always turns cold here at night.*

In his backpack, each has:
- *a large piece of foil,*
- *a large piece of waxed paper,*
- *a two-foot-long woolen scarf.*
- *There are three pine boughs nearby.*

3 *Take notes on how each person would prevent hypothermia (loss of body heat that can lead to death) from setting in?*

4 *How similar were the solutions?*

AMAZING NATIVE CULTURES

*Pyramid at Chichén Itzá,
Yucatan, Mexico*

When the first Europeans arrived in the Americas, they found civilizations there as complex as any of the so-called Old World (today's Europe and the Middle East).

Flat-topped pyramids and palaces in America were as large and dramatic as those of ancient Egypt or Europe. Ancient Native Americans knew about math, medicine, time, astronomy (studying the stars), and more.

A City Like No Other

Tenochtitlán

The glittering city of *Tenochtitlán* (ten-ohch-teet-LAHN), the great Aztec city in Mexico, was built on a land of lakes (in the place where Mexico City stands today). Bridges, canals, and causeways connected the city. There were palaces, aqueducts, flat-topped pyramids with plazas around them, marketplaces, and even floating gardens. Farms on the edge of the city produced more than enough food for the hundreds of thousands of people who lived there.

One Spaniard wrote that the marketplaces were "larger and better run than those of Rome or Constantinople," the greatest trading centers of the so-called Old World.

Even the man who conquered the city, Hernán Cortés (air-NAHN core-TESS), wrote home to say that the red-colored palaces of the Aztec king, *Montezuma* (mont-a-ZU-ma), were far more splendid than any castle in Spain.

Farther North

Adena serpent mound, Ohio, USA

North America, too, was filled with a variety of peoples, languages, and lifestyles long before Columbus arrived on its shores. Some, like the Mound Builders of the southeast, created incredible cities (Cahokia, Moundsville, and Etowah), with hundreds of flat-topped pyramids surrounded by well-built houses. They had fine possessions, too, because they used America's rivers to trade with people from as far west as present-day California and as far south as present-day Mexico.

Early North Americans, now called the *Adena*, constructed a quarter-mile long "snake" from tons of earth. Their beautiful artwork, made from mica, is as sleek as today's modern art.

The ancient southwestern ancestors of the Hopi constructed smooth, round rooms in a huge complex called Pablo Bonita in Chaco Canyon, New Mexico, in the United States.

Hot Cha Cha!

What did ancient languages sound like? Sample the sounds and beats of native languages by repeating this list of ancient South American cultures out loud several times in a row:

Olmec, Toltec, Mixtec, Aztec, Inca, Chichimec, Maya!

Do the same with words from North American tribes. They will sound very familiar.

Chicago, Massachusetts, Seattle, Idaho, Mississippi!

Internet Discovery
Don't miss this one:
<**www.mesoweb.com**>.

"FROM FOREVER WE HAVE BEEN HERE"

Lakota (Sioux) Chief

When did the ancestors of the Native Americans first arrive in the Americas? No one knows for sure, but some Native Americans have strong ideas about it. They write and speak about their beginnings with great beauty, grounded in the convictions from their unwavering belief.

THE LAKOTA THEORY ✳ ✳ ✳ ✳ ✳ ✳ ✳ ✳ ✳ ✳ ✳ ✳ ✳ ✳ ✳ ✳ ✳

"**O**ur elders taught that 'from forever we have been here.' Our first memory came from deep in the darkness of a cave. The cave was the womb of our Mother Earth, and it was a time when the Spirit of the Buffalo and the Spirit of Our Ancestors were One.

From our first breath came the Song of Our Hearts, seeking freedom from the darkness of the cave. Our Mother heard our cries for freedom, so she opened herself. She let the Buffalo People, our ancestors, move out of Wind Cave onto the Earth's surface in the Black Hills. From there they scattered to all directions of the Earth.

From forever we have been here. The life of all humans began here."

— *Charlotte Black Elk, a Lakota leader*

EVIDENCE *FOR* THE NATIVE STORIES ✻ ✻ ✻ ✻ ✻ ✻ ✻ ✻ ✻ ✻ ✻

• Native stories contain symbolism in the form of *metaphors*, a way of storytelling that uses one thing (for example, a bird) to represent another (for example, a spirit). Other times the stories contain actual truths. One example is a story about a whale that lived in a certain creek in the Northwest. Outsiders thought the traditional story was a symbolic tale. But in the 1960s, bones of a 10,000-year-old whale were found in the very creek mentioned in the story! How's that for proof?

• Although most experts agree that human life began in Africa, experts have been proven wrong many, many times throughout history.

Buffalo Dancer
After Awa Tsireh, about 1930–1940

Eagle Dancer
After Awa Tsireh, about 1917–1925

EVIDENCE *AGAINST* THE NATIVE STORIES ✻ ✻ ✻ ✻

• There is no scientific evidence for the native stories; they are based more in mythology than in scientific theory.

• In the Black Hills of Wyoming in the United States, no artifacts have been found in Wind Cave to support the Lakota Theory.

NATIVE ROOTS

Because native life has deep roots in America, native ideas show up in unusual places, like on United States money!

Find a one-dollar bill. Notice the eagle carrying a bundle of spears? In the native culture, the bundle stands for unity, meaning the more they stand together, the stronger the people of the United States will be.

But is that idea really true? Find out!

Try It!

Gather about a dozen dry sticks. Take one and snap it in two. How hard is it to break? Now bundle the other sticks together and try to break the bundle. How hard is that? What did you discover about unity, or working together, by doing this experiment?

Take the "Star Guide" Challenge!

Wow! We've visited a lot of theories about who really discovered America — all based on the ancient world. Take the *Star Guide Challenge*. Review the five fingers (see page 22) and the theories: Land-Bridge Theory (pages 23–25), Multiple-Migration Theory (page 32), King Woden-lithi Theory (pages 33–34), and Lakota Theory (pages 39–40).

Now, hang on to your results because there are many other theories to come.

THINK about it!

Rediscovering Ancient Beliefs

People who live close to nature share certain ideas that are spiritual and cannot be tested by science. For instance, native people believe planet Earth is alive. To them, the natural world is a living library. Along with books, they "read" rocks, water, grass, mountains, trees, animals, earth, and sky! Natives also believe that all life — animals, plants, and people — is connected in the great, living web of life. They believe that the fate of one is connected to the fate of the others.

Can you "read" nature? For example, do you know when a plant needs water or a tree is sick? If you were more "tuned in" to nature, what else might you notice?

Suppose you believed that every person, plant, and animal was a "relative" of yours. How would that change your actions and attitudes?

FANTASTIC ARCHAEOLOGY: HOW OPEN-MINDED ARE YOU?

Could the very first Americans have been space aliens, angels, or other beings from beyond? We admit, the ideas sound strange. But like other theories about America's discovery, this one has people who champion it. They put forward evidence needing investigation, too. And as Truth Trackers, keeping an open mind is a key to success, so before you write this off as nonsense, read on.

THE ALIEN THEORY * * * * * * *

In present day Nazca, Peru, and Blythe, California, something huge, mysterious, and very *real* exists. In those places, cut into the land are pictures of animals and humans, framed in huge triangles and trapezoids.

On the ground, the pictures don't look like much. To really see them, you have to go up. How far up? Very high! They can only be seen from the *sky!*

Aerial view of figure carved into land, Nazca, Peru

To some, this ancient earth art is evidence that people of the past communicated with beings from outer space. Some people think the pictures were created *for* aliens.

Some who hold to this theory believe that gifted aliens came to earth to marry the first apelike prehumans. From that union came intelligent human beings of today.

Brainstorm!

Brainstorming means coming up with many different ideas in an effort to find a solution to a tough problem. And there aren't many tougher questions than this one: Why would ancient people create pictures that can only be seen from the sky?

No one has answered that challenging question yet. But now that *you* are on the case, that situation may change!

Stretch your mind by trying to come up with some other explanations for the bird's view art. What are other possible reasons why the art was made?

Meet a Modern Explorer: *Erich von Daniken!*

Erich von Daniken is a Swiss writer who favors the Alien Theory. He knows that his ideas are highly unusual, but that hasn't stopped him from developing them. Von Daniken has written several books on the subject. The books are popular and read by intelligent people. Erich von Daniken is a good example of a person who is not afraid to think for himself.

Don't Be Ridiculous!

How accepting are you of way-out-there ideas? Do you immediately dismiss them? ("That is ridiculous!") Do you make fun of the person, rather than the idea? ("He's from another planet!") We all do this sometimes, either because the idea seems strange or sometimes because the idea actually scares us.

EVIDENCE *FOR* THE ALIEN THEORY * * * * * * * * * * * * * * *

• Von Daniken believes that stone pillars crafted by the Toltecs, a Mexican culture of the past, show astronauts armed with ray guns. (Look at the art on page 46 and see if you agree.) He also has found marks in the earth near the giant pictures that he says are from ancient rocket blasts, supporting his notion that aliens were involved.

• Around the world there are several mysterious rock structures that no one can fully explain. Across the United States, there are unexplained structures called *dolmans*, one giant stone held up by three small ones. The world-famous *Stonehenge*, with its giant pillars in a circle, is in England.

Stone structure at Mystery Hill, New Hampshire, USA, believed to be more than 4,000 years old.

EVISENCE *FOR* THE ALIEN THEORY (cont'd) * * * * * * * * * *

These structures baffled the best minds for years. How did ancient people move the stones, and why are they better seen from the sky? Later, experiments determined ways in which the structures might have been built through simple technology.

Still, by the Alien Theory, space creatures could have helped move the stones, would have appreciated their artistic qualities from above, and perhaps understood their true meaning.

Stonehenge, in Wiltshire, England:
What does this ancient structure mean?

Maybe it would work better over there...
No, wait! Maybe if...

• Then, there's the rock art of Canada (page 36) and elsewhere that contains pictures that look like an alien sky god. By the Alien Theory, the artists were copying something they had actually seen!

• Another piece of the puzzle that may fit the Alien Theory comes from the Mound Builders of the southeast United States (page 38). They told of a leader called "The Great Sun," who came directly from the sky to teach the people how to get along.

EVIDENCE *AGAINST* THE ALIEN THEORY *

Stone columns at the main temple in Toltec capital

Wild Ideas?

History is filled with stories of people who had strange or wild ideas that later proved to be accurate.

Coming up with new ideas — even far-out ones — is part of humanity's genius. It's important to listen to others, of course. Yet, if we blindly accept all their ideas and opinions, we risk losing the ability to make up our own minds.

Do you think for yourself? Or do you tend to follow other people's ideas?

Do you allow yourself time to make up your mind about things?

How far should we open our minds so that we are aware of other ideas, but not distracted by nonsense?

• Some people think von Daniken's ideas are brilliant and imaginative, but completely wrong. To them, the Toltec pillars show people holding farm tools or spears, not space weapons. They see his evidence of rocket blasts as evidence of an overactive imagination.

• As for the giant stone structures, well, they *are* mysterious. But perhaps prehistoric people had building technologies that we don't understand today. After all, the pyramids are massive stoneworks, too, though they're built of smaller individual stones, and they were definitely made by people — not aliens!

• Why must the art have come from aliens? Perhaps it was developed by ancient peoples who worshiped gods and goddesses or the forces of nature whom they believed lived in the sky. The art could be a gift for them.

MAKE A GIANT-SIZED DRAWING

If you knew that creatures who were out of this world would see your picture, what would you draw? A bike to show friendly aliens how to get around on planet Earth? A giant pizza for hungry aliens? A heart to show life? Use your imagination to come up with a simple image that sends a universal message so any person from anywhere could get its meaning.

YOU WILL NEED:

- *Paper*
- *Marker*
- *Ruler and yardstick*
- *Pebbles*
- *Large space, like a field, driveway, beach, or yard*
- *Long rope, chalk, or field-marking paint*

1 *Use an 8.5" by 11" (21 x 27.5 cm) piece of paper to draw the outline of the shape you want to make. Draw with a thick marker. Then, use the ruler to divide the paper into 12 blocks. (Space three lines down the paper and two across.)*

2 *Measure and mark (with pebbles) 8.5' by 11' (2.5 x 3.5 m) on the field. Create a grid by placing stones at the intersections of each square yard.*

3 *The paper grid is a map or guide for drawing. You translate each little piece into an expanded version, square by square. If you are using a driveway (with adult permission), use chalk.*

At the beach, sketch in the sand with a stick. On a lawn, try "drawing" with rope or yarn. Or use field-marking paint, the kind used on football fields.

4 *If you have a second-story window, view your creation from above.*

THE "WHY NOT?" DEPARTMENT

The "Why Not?" Department is an important – but imaginary – place where all possibilities are stored. Here are three events or legends that may offer clues about the original discovery of America. They are very old and may need a little dusting off, but they just might help you with a puzzle piece.

THE FALL OF CARTHAGE * * * * * * * * * * * * * * * * * *

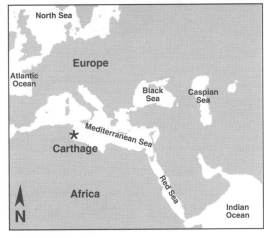

Ancient Carthage

When the African Empire of Carthage (in modern-day Libya, near Egypt) fell to the Romans (in about 200 B.C.), people had to flee.

Could they have fled to America? Hard evidence is lacking. But some experts point to the fact that the Carthaginians were especially capable sailors and that ocean currents flowed from ancient Carthage to America.

FROM ATLANTIS TO AMERICA * * * * * * * * * * * * * * * *

No one really knows if the legendary island of Atlantis that the Greek philosopher Plato wrote about actually existed. Some say it was an imaginary place; others believe it was an actual island located between Europe and America.

According to the legend, the people of Atlantis were peaceful and intelligent. When their beautiful island sank into the sea (perhaps in an earthquake), they had no choice but to flee.

Did they flee to America?

P.S. Which ocean did Atlantis supposedly sink into?

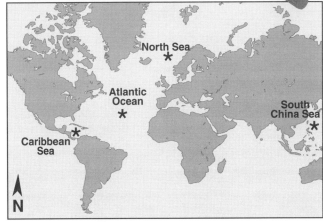

Various suggested sites of Atlantis

THE TEN LOST TRIBES OF ISRAEL ✳ ✳ ✳ ✳ ✳ ✳ ✳ ✳ ✳ ✳ ✳ ✳

When Columbus "discovered" America, the people of Europe were stunned! After all, the *Bible*, which supposedly told everything there is to know about history, never mentioned any other continents. How could such important information be missing?

Well, a closer reading of the *Bible* reveals a passage about 10 tribes of Israel that separated from the original 12 and were never heard of again.

Could the Ten Lost Tribes have made their way to America? That's what the Mormon religion teaches.

An Open Mind

Have you ever known someone who is so convinced about something that no new ideas can get into his head? The person is like a cup that is already full. Nothing more can fit into it!

Freeing your mind of old beliefs is tricky business. It sometimes means reaching new conclusions that don't agree with what you've been taught. Or it may mean having to wait for *more* information before deciding what to believe about something.

One thing is certain: An open mind is the most important tool for learning and discovery about any subject!

Try It!

Imagine an open mind. What symbols, shapes, images, and colors capture its meaning for you? Does it have a lot of layers? Does it look like something real or something abstract? Get some art materials (or write a poem), let yourself go, and be . . . open-minded!

Take the "Star Guide" Challenge!

How do the fantastic theories of this chapter hold up when you give them the *Star Guide* treatment? How do they compare with the less "far-out" ideas we explored earlier?

Which of the theories makes the most sense to you as you hunt for answers to the question, "Who *really* discovered America?"

THEY CROSSED THE BIG WATER
. . . PERHAPS!

L et's back track a little and ask a very basic question: Why has the assumption been made that the earliest true discovers of America could have only arrived by land. Couldn't the true discoverers have come by boat from Africa or Asia? Or, could it be that the Native Americans first went to Africa or Asia across the "Big Water"?

Given the long distances between continents and the fact that ancient people didn't have engine power, experts once doubted that the ancients could have made ocean-crossing journeys. *Obviously*, they would have starved or drowned before reaching America's shore. Right?

Let's see!

A Little Help From the Wind and Water

Imagine living in a world with no airplanes or large ships. You and your friends are standing at the shore, facing a huge ocean. You wonder what is across that water? Your friends wonder, too.

Soon, all of you want to find the answer. But how can you possibly travel over such a large distance? You sigh and think, "Wouldn't it be nice if there were conveyor belts in the ocean?"

Well, guess what — there are!

Conveyor Belts in the Ocean

If you've ever been to a large airport, you've probably walked onto a conveyor belt that moves travelers and their luggage along almost effortlessly. It is like a flat escalator or moving sidewalk.

The ocean has currents that are similar to conveyor belts. The currents are made by the natural action of wind and water working together. Strong currents become pathways, like long rivers flowing on the surface of the ocean. A ship that enters the current will move swiftly over the flowing water!

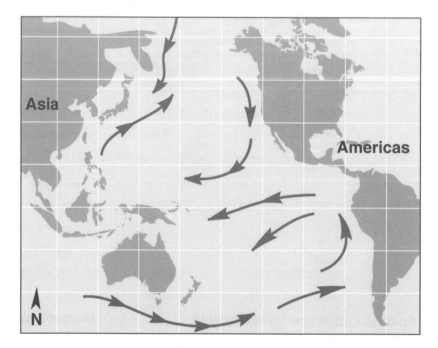

Ocean currents in the Pacific Ocean

Voyage of Ra II

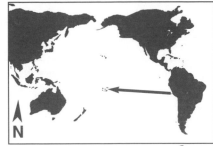

Voyage of
the Kon-Tiki

Meet A Modern Explorer: Thor Heyerdahl

Thor Heyerdahl is a Norwegian who moved to Polynesia (an island in the Pacific) to study ocean animals. There, a tribal chief taught him native ways. Fishing in Polynesia, as he had been taught, Heyerdahl often struggled against strong easterly winds that threatened to carry his boat away.

One day, he was struck with an idea: What would happen if the boat simply followed the flow of the water? How far would the wind and water take him? He began to wonder: Did ancient people sail the oceans propelled by ocean currents?

Experts told him that the idea was impossible, but that didn't stop Heyerdahl. He decided to use a powerful tool of historians: *re-enactment*. He would make a replica of an ancient reed boat, get some friends together to sail it, and see how far the ocean currents would take them!

Heyerdahl made three voyages in primitive-style vessels named *Kon-Tiki, Ra I,* and *Ra II.* Sailing under a flag of the United Nations, he and his crew ate fish that they caught along the way and collected rainwater to drink.

Two out of three of his voyages were successful. The *Kon-Tiki* took them from Peru to Polynesia. The *Ra II* brought them from Africa to Barbados in the Caribbean.

Because Thor Heyerdahl followed his hunch, the idea of ancient ocean travel went from being *obviously* impossible to being a real possibility!

MAKE A REED BOAT

People of the ancient past built boats from tall reeds. The reeds were bundled together and dried to build ships capable of sailing from continent to continent — especially on ocean currents.

1 *To make a reed-style boat, cut and collect plenty of tall grass or straw. (If it's green, you'll have to let it dry out before using it.)*

2 *Bundle bunches of it with twine to make several long strips.*

3 *Tie the strips together in the shape of a banana. (Round off the edges by tying them back.)*

4 *To add a passenger seat, insert a slender rectangle of cardboard into the middle of the boat. Bon voyage!*

Perhaps They Came from Africa

In 1897, a Mexican farmer was digging in his garden when he hit a huge boulder. Curious, he began digging around it.

After some digging, to his amazement — and the amazement of the whole world! — he saw that the boulder was actually a statue of a colossal 20-ton head! (See page 56.) And with this find and similar ones that followed began a great debate that as yet is unresolved.

People not only wondered who could have constructed such enormous heads, but they were further baffled by the images of the heads which, to some, appeared to have some Negroid features. Had people from Africa crossed the Atlantic Ocean and been to the Americas as early as 2,000 years before Columbus? Or, did native peoples of the Americas simply share those same features?

How in the world did a sculpture of what may be an African person's head come to be found in America? Let's investigate!

Big Statues

The dozens of Olmec sculpted heads are enormous! They are said to weigh between 20 and 40 tons each, be dark-colored, and be carved from a type of rock called basalt. They are described by many as having Negroid features and they appear to be wearing helmets that may have been worn in a type of ball game believed to have been played at that time.

Do you think a large statue means the subject is more important to a culture than a small statue is? Or does it mean the subject is more feared? Idolized? Or is it just the style of art popular in that culture or time? If statue size matters, what is important in our American cultures today?

Obviously, It's an African . . . Or Not.

• *Did an African sculpt an African in America?* That would mean that Africans had actually settled here long enough to build these massive sculptures.

• *Did an Olmec (a native cultural group that lived in this area) sculpt Africans?* That would mean that Africans had been here and had been observed by the Olmec, unless, of course, it was the other way around (see page 62), and the Olmec sailed to Africa, observed Africans, and returned, building these sculptures then.

• *Did an Olmec sculpt an Olmec?* That's a good question since there are those who believe that some of the Olmec may have shared certain features with those from Africa. Thus, they sculpted themselves.

Olmec head, Mexico

The questions are endless and exciting, too. Even the experts whom we have been turning to can't come to consensus, or agreement, about the role the Africans may have played in the discovery of America. So, it is up to you, Truth Tracker, to try to shed some light on the controversy.

Disagreement is a good thing:
It makes us all dig deeper, think harder,
and strive for open-minded discussion.

We are alerting you right now: Some scholars call some of these theories "hogwash," "pure bunk," "old ideas that are no longer widely held." Of course, for every opinion like that, others say, "Amazing!" "Finally some real evidence!" and "Another piece of the puzzle is solved."

So, What's a Truth-Tracking Kid Supposed to Believe?

Well, kiddo, we've come upon a big, big problem that just doesn't seem to have an *obvious* answer. In this case, evidence that proves something to one group of researchers seems unlikely to others. Each group researches the evidence and comes to different, but *feasible* (that means possible) conclusions. So we are left to do what we have been doing throughout this adventure: We have to use our tracking tools to assess the theories and the evidence. That way we can reach a conclusion that seems best to us, for now.

But, before you proceed, Truth Tracker, make sure you still have those valuable tools with you: your *open mind* (the one that let you look at the Alien Theory without immediately calling it foolish); the *sharp pickax* that allows you to pick through the rubble of time and prejudices to get closer to the truth; and the *bright light* to shine on those little specks of wisdom that may come darting across your mind like a shooting star. With those tools front and center, you will have everything you need to *listen to the theories, evaluate the evidence,* and *reach your own conclusions.*

Here then are some of these controversial theories.

The Olmec: A Native People

The colossal statue was part of what is called the Olmec culture. The Olmec lived from about 1200 B.C. to about A.D. 600 along the Gulf Coast in present-day Mexico. Some think they were early farmers of a corn-like crop (but no kernels or hard evidence of this has ever been found) who supplemented their diet by fishing and hunting. Usually, they are thought of as the ones who set the groundwork for the great American cultures that followed. They developed a calendar; they had a kind of writing; and their religion honored a jaguar and serpent-shaped image.

Olmec images

Some experts believe that the Olmec culture was actually made up of smaller groups with their own language, social system, and beliefs. These experts believe that the Olmec region was too large for a single culture. But however you view these people — as a single culture or several grouped together — they were *indigenous* (which means they were always here). And that is the point to tuck away as we continue: Were the Olmec a culture resulting from their own ingenuity, ideas and creativity, or were they influenced by others who had been here before them?

Meet A Modern Explorer: Dr. Ivan Van Sertima

Dr. Ivan Van Sertima, a Rutgers University professor, writes about African influence in ancient America. A native of Guyana, Africa, Professor Van Sertima has written, "What I have sought to prove is not that Africans 'discovered' America, but that they made contact on at least a half a dozen occasions, two of which are culturally significant (important)."

His ideas certainly are controversial! Many have completely discredited Professor Van Sertima's theories about Africans arriving in the Americas before the Olmec culture evolved. They say that the enormous heads carved by the Olmec are based on Olmec people, not Africans. These experts don't believe there were any Africans living in America so early.

VAN SERTIMA'S AFRICAN THEORY * * * * * * * * *

Professor Van Sertima believes that the first Africans arrived in America almost 2,000 years before Columbus, when the Olmec civilization was beginning. These Africans were not slaves. Instead, they were highly respected traders, leaders, and *shamans* (high priests or priestesses). According to the professor, they introduced new ideas, new foods, and new customs to the native people. He says that because of this African influence, the Native American culture developed into one of the world's great early cultures, the Olmec.

EVIDENCE *FOR* THE AFRICAN THEORY * * *  * *

Egyptian pyramid at Giza, Egypt. Compare it with the flat-topped pyramids believed to have been built by the Olmec (see page 37).

Professor Van Sertima believes that the Olmec culture was influenced by Africans from *Nubia* (NOO-be-ah), an ancient African land. He gives these examples as evidence:

• Picture writing in an Egyptian pyramid tells of a westward voyage organized by a pharaoh in about 1200 B.C.

• Olmec royalty wore a double crown, just as the Africans did.

• The Olmec built pyramids, worshiped cats (jaguars), and created colossal statues, just as the Africans did.

• Olmec gods were part human and part animal, like African gods.

• The Olmec used picture writing, called *hieroglyphics*, as did the Africans.

• Columbus writes that the Taino (see page 78) told him about dark-skinned people who came from the East.

EVIDENCE *AGAINST* THE AFRICAN THEORY

Stone "Moai" statues on the slopes of Easter Island

Many experts disagree with Professor Van Sertima, saying that he has no real proof for his ideas.

• Critics argue that the huge stone heads resemble the local (indigenous) people, not Africans. They say the statues are dark because volcanic stone from the Toosala Mountains was the most readily available.

• They say that the flat-topped Olmec pyramids are not like Egyptian pyramids.

• Critics say that colossal statues have been seen in other parts of the world, such as Easter Island, and are not just African.

• Supernatural beings that are part human and part animal are found in almost every human society where shamanism is important, not just in Africa.

• The sightings reported by the Taino people were probably of people with darker skin, not necessarily Africans.

THINK about it!

The Thing about Evidence

You've probably heard of circumstantial evidence in movies and TV detective stories. It's evidence that seems to support the idea that something happened, but there is no real proof. Historical evidence can be circumstantial; it can also be misused (purposely misleading); or it can be misconstrued (misinterpreted so that it seems to say one thing, but could also be used to say another).

Does Professor Van Sertima's evidence prove his theory to you?

Do you think that the same evidence could be used to support other theories?

What do *you* think about the idea that Africans may have sailed to America so long ago?

PROFESSOR XU'S ASIAN THEORY ✳ ✳ ✳ ✳ ✳

Professor Mike Xu, of the University of Central Oklahoma, believes that refugees from the Chinese Shang dynasty influenced the development of the Olmec civilization.

EVIDENCE *FOR* THE ASIAN THEORY ✳  ✳

- The timing is perfect. Soon after the Shang dynasty was defeated, causing people to flee, the Olmec culture began.
- There are 150 photos of Olmec *glyphs* (writing) that Professor Xu believes closely resemble ancient Chinese writing.
- A mysterious jade sculpture called *Offering #4* that was found in La Venta, a dug-out Olmec city, contains glyphs that Professor Xu believes resemble ancient Chinese writing and tell about people establishing a kingdom.

EVIDENCE *AGAINST* THE ASIAN THEORY

Professor Xu's theory has also eluded proof.
- Professor Xu believes that the Olmec glyphs resemble ancient Chinese, but many disagree. They believe the Olmec language resembles the Mixe-Zoque language, a native language that is completely different from Chinese.
- Scholars have not been able to confirm Professor Xu's interpretation of the writing and story of *Offering #4.*

THE OTHER WAY-AROUND THEORY ✳ ✳

By this way of thinking, ancient people from the Americas took to the ocean and sailed on currents to Africa, Asia, or Europe. They may have helped create the great cultures of Egypt or China. They may have influenced ancient Europeans, too. (After all, why does every theory have discoverers coming from elsewhere to America?)

Evidence has been found in Canada and Sweden of a Red Paint People, who used iron dust in their burials. According to carbon dating, artifacts of the Red Paint People from North America are older than the ones from Sweden. Also, some experts point to the stone tools that have been found in California: They are believed to be from 200,000 years ago — that's 194,000 years before the Egyptians built the pyramids!

Turn the Puzzle Around!

Come on, Truth Tracker! Let's turn convention – the way people usually think of something – on its ear. Like turning a picture or puzzle around for a fresh look, let's ask if America was the place where cultures first began! Maybe it was the native peoples from the Americas like the Olmec who "discovered" Europe and Africa!

Matching Artifacts

Did you ever play with a pull toy when you were a toddler? Then, you have something in common with kids of the ancient past. Pull toys have been found in ancient Africa, ancient Asia, and ancient America! So, have soul houses, which are miniature clay or wooden houses. Also, pyramids existed in both America and Africa.

We won't be alone in exploring this idea, either. Plenty of professionals are investigating that possibility right now! And why not? The ocean currents don't flow in only one direction. The native peoples were extremely capable in building their cities and establishing sophisticated cultures. So, why would we not consider that events happened the other way around?

Did each culture invent these things on its own, separately and independently of each other? Or did they get started in one place and spread through human contact? These are two very basic questions of archaeology – with no certain answers yet. What is *your* opinion? (Review your experiment on page 35.)

Take the "Star Guide" Challenge!

If all these theories have you longing for a little certainty, let's make our way to North America in a later age. But first update your *Star Guide* (see page 22) with the theories described on pages 51–63. Then, turn the page where we will find evidence of a "discovery" that *definitely* occurred about 1,000 years ago!

THE VIKINGS "DISCOVERED" AMERICA!

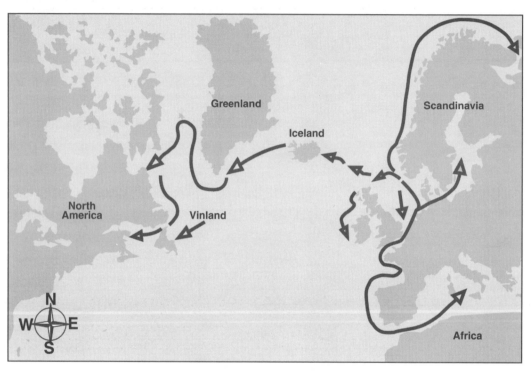

The Vikings' routes to America

The Vikings (also called Norse, Nordic, and Northmen) are the ancestors of today's Scandinavians. Unlike other ideas about early arrivals to America (including the one about Norse ancestor King Woden-lithi, page 33), visits by the Vikings, which we are about to explore, have moved from theory to fact.

P.S. A good way to remember the Scandinavian countries is to think of the archaeological term "finds": **F**inland, **I**celand, **N**orway, **D**enmark, and **S**weden.

THE VIKINGS: RAIDERS AND TRADERS OF THE OPEN SEAS

Viking knorr

*I*n the cold lands of northern Europe, with short growing seasons, people of the past had to be creative to survive. And some would say the Vikings became a little *too* creative. They raided other lands to get survival goods! (The word "Viking" is the Norse word for pirate.)

Two or three Viking ships, each with about 50 men, would sail to other lands. They'd pull into the harbor and run ashore, screaming, with their swords raised high. Then, they'd steal whatever they wanted!

But the Norse were much more than bullies. They were among the first people to practice democracy and to respect the rights of women. Many were peaceful traders who sailed the oceans, exchanging goods and finding treasures to bring back home. In their open boats, called *knorrs*, they went all the way to Rome and parts of the Middle East — and also to North America.

Examining the Evidence: Sagas and Oop-Art

There are two kinds of evidence that prove the Norse actually traveled to America: oop-art and *sagas* (long stories or legends about people or events in history).

For over 900 years, only the sagas existed, making the Norse visits theory, not fact. Then, in the 1960s, all sorts of Norse oop-art were found in Canada. (More about that later!)

Saga Stars

Like modern-day movies, sagas are stories that tell how people of the past faced difficulty and overcame it. The first sagas were spoken, passed down from parent to child to keep history alive. Then, in the tenth century, the stories were written down. Today, they exist as old documents.

The first saga to mention the "discovery" of America is the story of *Bjarni* (bee-ARN-ee) *Herulfson*. But it turns out that Bjarni wasn't looking for a new world at all!

The First Saga: Bjarni's Journey

Bjarni Herulfson had a fine knorr — as big as a house — and a friendly crew to help him sail it. He made his living as a global trader, traveling to foreign lands, exchanging goods, and collecting treasure. Every spring and summer, Bjarni went to work at sea. But in winter, when the seas were too cold to sail, he returned to Iceland to "enjoy the quiet company" of his dad, Herulf.

In the winter of 985, Bjarni returned from sea only to find that his father had moved to Greenland with his friend *Erik the Red*, who was starting a colony there.

Bjarni and his crew set sail for Greenland, but a fierce storm set in. Thunder raged, and a dense fog hung over the sky for days, hiding the stars that Bjarni needed to help him navigate.

When the fog lifted, Bjarni spied land with rolling hills and lots of trees. He knew it could not be Greenland because it had no glaciers. The crew wanted to go ashore to get fresh water and firewood. But Bjarni said they still had plenty of those things on board! (Since Bjarni was the captain, they did as he said and turned around.)

Sailing east, Bjarni finally spotted land with a huge glacier. Pulling into the harbor at dusk, he broke out in a grin when he saw his father waving to him. (The place where they met is called *Herulfsness* today!)

Bjarni got what he wanted, the quiet company of his dad. And oh, by the way, that land with rolling hills he had spotted earlier was North America!

The Second Saga: Leif Eriksson "Discovered" America in the year 1000!

When Bjarni returned home, he told his friend "Lucky Leif" about the land he had spotted. (Leif was called "Lucky" ever since he had pulled eight drowning sailors out of the sea, but that's another saga!) The son of Erik the Red, who colonized Greenland, Leif had discovery in his blood.

Leif was ever so curious about this new land of rolling hills. It took a few years, but he finally bought Bjarni's old knorr and headed westward! When he found the land, he liked it so much that he called it "Vinland the Good." He found salmon "bigger than any ever seen." He found good wheat and hardwood, too. Best of all, it was free for the taking! After a few months, Leif headed home with samples of Vinland's riches. That made others curious about Vinland, too.

Did Bjarni Discover America?

By the dictionary definition, it's accurate to say that Bjarni discovered America because he "espied" it, meaning he saw it (see page 11). Putting aside other theories for a moment, do you count his adventure as a true discovery? Do you think that just *seeing* something is meaningful enough? Or do you think that people have to *do* something about whatever it is they see to claim it as a true discovery?

MAKE A KNORR

Viking knorrs were the most seaworthy ships of their time. Made from oak, with woolen sails, knorrs had graceful curved ends carved into the shape of a huge animal that would supposedly keep evil spirits away!

Sailors rowed their knorrs by sitting on wooden chests containing their personal belongings.

YOU WILL NEED:

- *Bowl of water*
- *Popsicle sticks*
- *Scissors*
- *Waxed juice carton*

- *Cereal-box cardboard*
- *Duct or masking tape*
- *Aluminum foil*
- *Glue*
- *Steel wool*
- *Paints and paintbrushes*
- *Drinking straw*

- *Wooden dowel (or chopstick)*
- *3" (7.5 cm) square cloth (or construction paper)*
- *Twine (or string)*
- *Round cardboard discs (or construction paper discs)*

Squeeze together and tape

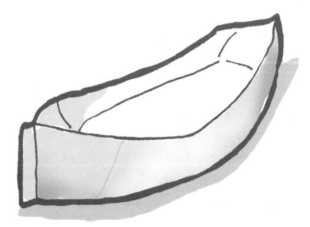

1 *First, get a bowl of water and soak the Popsicle sticks. Then, cut off one long side of the juice carton on three sides, leaving the bottom attached. Trim the bottom flap, and roll it tightly to make a curved stern (rear of the ship).*

2 *Bend the rest of the carton to make the knorr as curved as possible. Trim the sides to make them lower.*

3 The triangular end will be the bow (front of the ship), showing an animal's head on a long neck. From the cardboard, cut two identical animal profiles with necks about 8" (20 cm) long. Tape the "face" of both strips together and put crushed foil between them (in the neck.) Attach the entire head to the inside of the knorr.

4 Gently bend the soaked sticks until they are slightly curved. When they dry, glue them to the sides of the ship. Scratch the waxed surface of the ship with steel wool and paint the knorr. Cover the animal head and neck with the dull side of the foil.

5 In the middle of the bottom of the knorr, pool some glue and stick in the drinking straw. (A few pieces of chewed bubble gum or a lump of clay might help it to stay up, too.)

6 For the sail, glue a 3" (7.5 cm) square piece of cloth to a stick. Attach the sail to the straw with twine taped to the stick, leaving enough twine on each side as rigging, the ropes that helped the Vikings steer.

7 Glue round cardboard discs to the sides of the ship to resemble the sailors' shields. Your knorr will be seaworthy — well, "bathtub-worthy" — for a few hours at least!

WRITE (OR ACT OUT) A SAGA

How about writing or acting out a saga about yourself and the people around you?

1 *Tell the life story of a grandparent, for instance. Put the high points and the low points of life into your saga, and be very dramatic! Your saga can even stretch the truth a little, as the old sagas sometimes did.*

Rrr-ipp!

2 *Norse sagas were written on parchment, which is paper made from lambskin. Write yours on a crumpled grocery bag or white paper dipped in tea. Tear the edges to make it look old.*

The Saga Continues: 162 Vikings "Discover" America!

Luckily Leif had a sister-in-law, *Gudrid*, who was married to trader *Thorfinn Karlsnefi*. Gudrid and Thorfinn made a deal with Leif to set up a family business in Vinland and share the profits with him.

In 1010, Gudrid, Thorfinn, and 160 others took off for Vinland. They packed wisely, bringing some iron ember hearths (small metal boxes that kept chunks of wood burning during the day when a big fire was not needed), hand-held spindles to weave yarn out of wool, warm cloaks with metal fasteners to keep the cold out, and nails and tools for ship building.

When they arrived, Gudrid knelt and lapped up the dew, which was "sweeter than anything" she had ever tasted.

The Norse built a settlement and began trading with the natives, whom they called *skraelings*. Gudrid gave birth to a baby boy, *Snorri*, the first Viking born on American soil!

Meet Modern Explorers: *Helge and Anne Ingstad*

Until the 1960s, no one had known for sure if the Norse sagas were fact or fiction (a made-up story). A couple of curious Norwegians decided to find out. Using clues found in the sagas, Helge and Anne Ingstad began to search for the land Leif had described.

They searched Rhode Island and Massachusetts in the United States, and Nova Scotia, Canada, asking everyone they met about possible Viking ruins. People just shrugged, unable to provide any information.

One day, Helge took a day trip on a fishing boat visiting villages in Newfoundland, Canada. Prepared for disappointment once again, he nevertheless asked his usual question about possible Viking ruins. But this time the man he asked scratched his head and said there might be something up at "Lancey Meadow."

Lancey Meadow turned out to be *L'Anse aux Meadows.* When Helge arrived at the place, he immediately noticed that it matched the saga's description of Vinland *perfectly!*

Could he have finally found Vinland the Good? Helge called his wife and excitedly told her the news!

Oop-art by the Dozen!

The dig was on. The Ingstads' first find was an iron ember hearth. Since Native Americans did not have iron, chances were excellent that it was a Norse artifact.

Then came the discovery of eight building foundations, followed by shipbuilding nails, a Norse cloak fastener, and a spindle. Remember Gudrid's saga (page 70)? This oop-art added up to *proof* that the Norse had actually been there!

Internet Discovery

To see pictures of the Vikings in America, check out The Norse at the Canada Hall website at <**www.civilization.ca/c mc/cmceng/ca01eng .html**>

GROW A HOUSE

The Viking houses in America were made of living green walls called sod. *Sod walls are great at keeping bad weather out and cozy comfort in. Each house had a skylight that let light in and smoke out. You, too, can make a sod house.*

YOU WILL NEED:

- *2 florist foam blocks (4" x 7"/10 x 17.5 cm)*
- *Rubber bands*
- *Craft knife*

- *7 Popsicle sticks*
- *Glue*
- *Cereal-box cardboard*
- *Scissors*
- *Bobby pins (or florist pins)*
- *Reindeer moss*

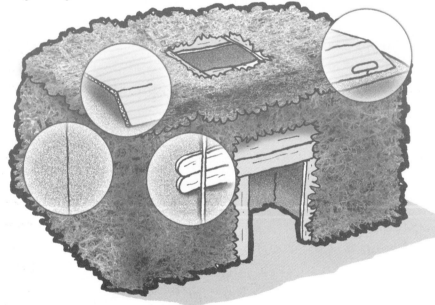

1 *Attach the foam blocks together with the rubber bands. To make a door, use a craft knife to dig out an opening in the foam. Make a door frame from Popsicle sticks, gluing on the upright sticks first. Place the ends of the top stick under the rubber bands.*

2 *To make the roof, fold the cardboard horizontally to fit. Cut out a small, square smoke hole in the middle of the roof. Frame it with glued-on pieces of stick.*

3 *Use pins to attach the roof to the blocks. Attach the moss with pins or glue, starting on the roof and working down. To keep the moss fresh, spritz it lightly with water after the glue has dried.*

And the Saga Goes On —

Do you wonder what happened to the Vikings in America? Then, read on as the saga concludes with a tale of action, adventure, and a terrible culture clash!

Reproduction of Viking sod house, Newfoundland, Canada

One day, a Viking bull escaped its pen and ran bellowing into the skraeling camp! The terrified skraelings, who had never seen such a beast, tried to run to safety inside the sod house.

But seeing the skraelings racing toward them frightened the Vikings. They barred the doors to keep them out!

After that incident, the Vikings built a tall wall around their settlement. But the skraelings ignored it! When they arrived at the Viking camp with furs to trade the following spring, the skraelings simply tossed their packs over the fence and climbed over.

At this point, the Vikings decided to move to another location. They took Snorri and all the others to set up another trading business with different skraelings.

One night after they had moved, Gudrid sat rocking Snorri's cradle. Suddenly "there was a crash" — a Northman had killed a skraeling for "stealing" a sword!

Thorfinn knew the skraelings would be back to avenge the murder. He and his men got their weapons ready. What a battle erupted the next day! The saga says, "the skraelings hurtled a large blue sphere" over the wall. It "hit the ground with a terrible din," terrifying the Vikings, who had never seen or heard anything like it!

With that, the Vikings started packing. This time they left Vinland the Good — for good!

And so, America remained a land of native cultures for 500 more years.

Culture Clashes

Imagine if the Vikings and skraelings had learned to understand each other. The Norse and the natives might have created a different America, changing history forever!

Without understanding other cultures and traditions, things can easily go wrong. The natives didn't respect the wall built by the Norse, for instance, because they had lived on that land for ages. The ideas of "private property" and "personal possessions" were not part of their world.

When the native took the Northman's sword, he was probably "taking his turn" with a new, exotic item, since native people shared all they had, borrowing freely from each other. If the Northman had understood this, he might not have killed the native. Likewise, the native might not have taken the sword if he had understood Norse ways.

People of today have culture clashes, too. Is there a culture that you don't understand? Maybe the culture of boys seems strange to a girl, or vice versa! Maybe the ways of older people and younger people seem to clash. Maybe people who live in rural areas think that city life is scary. Yet, city people may find country life scary!

When we put aside our fears of what is new or different, it becomes clear: There are many different ways to live in this world!

The Big Blue Sphere

Do you wonder about the big blue sphere that the natives hurled into the Viking camp? What the weapon was is lost in history. But it certainly was effective! The Native Americans thoroughly defeated the newcomers, running them right off the continent!

WHAT HAPPENED TO THE VIKINGS?

Norse descendants still live in Scandinavia. Some Vikings raided France and found it so nice that they settled there. They became the "Normans" of Normandy, France. Others settled in the cities of Dublin, Ireland, and York, England. Some went to Scotland, and others settled in Russia. (There's another one of those oop-words, again: "Russ" means red, from the redheaded Vikings.)

When the Vikings tried to attack the ancient Egyptians, however, they were repelled and had to flee. They got as far as Libya, where they stayed on, becoming the blue-eyed Berbers of Arabia today!

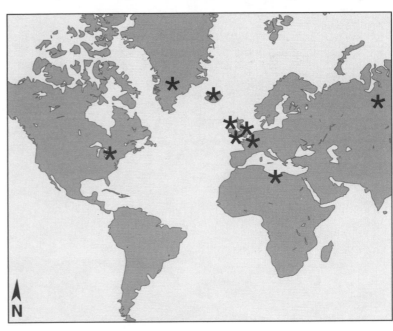

Where the Vikings settled

Take the "Star Guide" Challenge!

Where does a saga end and history begin? That's the question the Ingstads tried to answer. Put your *Star Guide* to the test and see how these Viking sagas weigh in.

WHAT DO YOU THINK?

Well, Truth Tracker, what's your opinion about the Viking "discovery" of America? How close do their actions come to answering the question that our book asks?

And while we're asking, why do you think there is so much new interest in the Norse in America? Perhaps, the reason has something to do with Columbus's changing place in history.

So, it seems our search for answers is not finished yet! Turn the page to enter the time that has come to be called the Age of Discovery. Let's find out what Columbus's discovery was really all about!

Columbus "Discovered" America!

THE FIRST VOYAGE

Return track

Outward-bound track

Bahamas

Cuba

Hispaniola

N

ATLANTIC OCEAN

Africa

Portugal

Spain

Returned March 15, 1493

Departed August 3, 1492

"In 1492, Columbus sailed the ocean blue."
school song from the 1950s

Everyone has heard the name Christopher Columbus! Thousands of cities, schools, roads, and buildings are named for him — even the country of Colombia is!

But who was Columbus, really? Was he a brave explorer who ventured to new lands, opening the doors of opportunity? Or was he an evil exploiter who harmed innocent people just to make himself rich?

We will soon discover that, like all people, Columbus was not all good or all bad, but somewhere in between. Just as in the story of America's discovery, there are many layers to this man and his experiences and many different ways to understand his accomplishments.

Still, for a long time, the story of Columbus's adventure was told as a simple tale, the one your parents and grandparents probably learned at school. Some people still believe it is the truth, but you may choose to see it differently!

Christopher Columbus: The Simple Story

Once, a daring *young Italian* named Christopher Columbus set out to find the rich lands of the east, the Indies (which then included India, Japan, China, and the islands of the East Indies). He wanted to bring their gold, jewels, and spices back to his homeland.

Now in those days, *everyone believed that the world was flat* – except Columbus! He did not fear falling off planet Earth's edge or being eaten by monsters. Columbus decided to go where no one had ever gone, sailing west in order to reach the East.

He asked several kings for money for the adventure, but they turned him down. Finally, Queen Isabella and King Ferdinand of Spain agreed to help. *Isabella pawned her jewels* to raise the money to buy him three ships: the *Niña*, the *Pinta*, and the *Santa Maria*.

Columbus sailed west and spent weeks on the open sea. His crew became fearful and angry. *They wanted to throw Columbus overboard!*

Finally, *on October 12, 1492, Columbus spied land! He went ashore with a Spanish flag, claiming the land for Spain.* Since he thought he was in the area of the East Indies, *he called the small group of people that he met, Indians.* These *primitive* people had never seen strangers before. *Some thought Columbus was a god!*

Columbus had discovered America! *He became a hero for all time!*

Hot! Hot! Hot! or Brrr!: Hunt For the Truth

Let's look at the Columbus story to discover what's hot (closer to the truth) and what's not (further from the truth).

1 *"Everyone believed that the earth was flat."*

Cold! The ancient Greeks had already figured out that planet Earth was a sphere. All educated people of Columbus's day knew this.

2 *"Columbus was a young Italian."*

Warm. Columbus was 39 years old when he crossed the Atlantic. As for being Italian, he grew up in Italy, but mysteriously, always spoke and wrote in Spanish. Some believe he came from a family of Spanish Jews, but he was born in Genoa, Italy.

3 *"Isabella pawned her jewels to finance his trip."*

Brrr! Freezing! Columbus's ships and crew cost about the same as two banquets (big parties). No hardship there! Let's not feel sorry for Queen Isabella!

4 *"The crew wanted to throw Columbus overboard!'*

Hot! Hot! Hot! Columbus had to promise his crew that they would turn back if they didn't see land by October 14. (He sure cut it close!)

5 *"On October 12, 1492, Columbus saw land!"*

Very, very hot! He spied a flickering light on the evening of October 11, but decided to wait until morning to go ashore.

6 *"He went ashore with a flag, claiming the land for Spain."*

Hot! Hot! Hot! All the Europeans who came after Columbus repeated this flag ritual, too.

7 *"Columbus met a small group of people and called them Indians."*

Pretty hot. But on the cooler side, the small group he met represented hundreds of thousands of others who lived on the island or near it. Their name for themselves was *Taino* (tah-EE-no).

8 *"The primitive natives had never seen strangers before."*

Freezing! Icicles everywhere! Primitive? The "Indians" had plenty to eat and lived in homes with nice possessions. They were experienced traders.

9 *"Some thought Columbus was a god."*

Freezing! Icicles everywhere! The Taino had their own name for their god *Atabey* (a-TAH-bay) and their own way of worshiping. They were happy with their religion. Columbus may have wanted to be worshiped and idolized, but he wasn't.

10 *"Columbus became a hero for all time!"*

Lukewarm. Columbus was more or less forgotten just a few years after his journey. In Spain, his assistant, Martin Pinzon, got as much, if not more glory for the "discovery" as Columbus did. (In Spain, they still celebrate Pinzon Day, but not Columbus Day!) In 1507, the new lands were named "America" for the discoverer of the South America mainland, *Amerigo Vespucci* (vez-PEW-chee). Columbus only regained his fame in the 1920s when Italian-American immigrants seeking a hero established Columbus Day.

PROVE IT FOR YOURSELF

How did the ancient Greeks figure out that planet Earth was really round? Get a globe (or any round object) and an object with some height (like a pencil or toy sailboat) to find out.

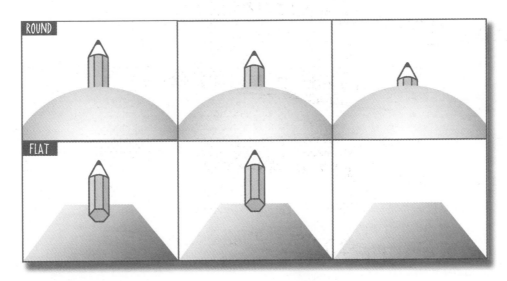

1 Hold the globe at eye level. Then, in slow and steady motion, move the pencil along the surface as if it were a ship at sea. Notice the way it slowly disappears from view as it moves away from you.

2 Do the same on a flat surface (like a book). Notice how it disappears this time. What is the difference? (See the answer below.)

Answer: On round objects, the "ship" disappears a little at a time, until the top of the sail finally sinks from view as it moves away from you. On flat surfaces, the drop is fast and dramatic!

COLUMBUS: CLOSER TO THE TRUTH

Okay, Truth Tracker! Now, let's explore some deeper layers of Columbus's story to ferret out facts and unearth information that will bring us closer to the truth.

A SEAMAN AND HIS AMAZING IDEA

Cristofo Columbo (his real name) was born in Genoa, Italy, to hard-working parents who lived near the sea. At 14, he took a job on a ship delivering cheese to Italian ports. His career as a seaman had begun.

When Columbus was 25, pirates attacked a ship that he was working on. Hundreds of sailors drowned that day, but Columbus managed to cling to a piece of wood that carried him to shore near Lisbon, Portugal. His brother was living there and working as a *cartographer*, a person who makes maps and sea charts. Columbus became a cartographer, too.

Meeting seamen from many lands brought opportunity, and Columbus soon found a job sailing to England and Iceland. (A piece of the puzzle? Maybe while there, he heard about the Vikings' adventures in Vinland.)

At 28, Columbus married, had a son, Diego, and began a business sailing to islands of the Atlantic. There, old sailors showed him carved wood that had floated in from the West.

That's when an amazing idea took shape in Columbus's mind. Since the world was round, he realized, the *East* — and all the treasures and wealth of the Indies — could be reached by sailing *west*! Now that may be Columbus's most clear and creative thinking ever!

THE DREAM COMES TRUE

Columbus's wife died at a young age, leaving him a single father. The grieving seaman brought young Diego to Spain to live at a monastery. There, a monk became a friend, introducing Columbus to people who knew Queen Isabella.

Columbus offered the queen a plan. *If* his idea about the new route was true, then incredible riches would come to her and Spain. To reward his risk, he asked for the titles of admiral and governor of any lands he discovered, along with a 10 percent share of any profits. (Quite a businessman!) He also agreed to spread the Catholic religion on behalf of the queen.

Isabella listened, but finally turned him away. That rainy day, Columbus left her castle on a mule, a defeated man. But his luck changed when a messenger caught up with him to say the queen had changed her mind!

So, in August 1492, after 10 years of rejection from kings, queens, and the wealthy, Columbus set sail with high hopes of finding wealth and power!

BE A CARTOGRAPHER

Imagine making a map or a chart of a place you had never been! How would you do it? That is exactly the situation that cartographers faced in Columbus's time. Seamen would describe the land and waterways they had encountered, and the cartographers would try to draw them.

1 *Get a friend or two and try making some maps of your own. Take turns describing the route to a place that one of you knows, but the others don't. For example, "My grandmother lives in the next town. To get there, I go out of my driveway and turn left. Then, I go onto a highway for a long time. When I see a shopping center at a stoplight, I turn left, etc." As you speak, your friend draws.*

2 *Then, switch roles. If you don't know the exact way, that's fine. Just put in lots of landmarks that you pass. Now, try following the map (with an adult, of course). Where do you end up?*

Welcome to Paradise

Imagine sunny skies, sandy shores, and sparkling, clear water! Then, imagine red parrots flying through the air. Pretty nice! You wouldn't have to imagine it if you were on a Caribbean island — which is where Columbus and his men first came ashore in America.

There, the natives lived happily in nature. Columbus wrote: "Better land and better people cannot be found. Their houses and villages are so pretty, and they have the sweetest speech. They love their neighbors as themselves. And they are gentle and always laughing."

Columbus reasoned that this had to be an island off the coast of Japan or China! But where were the gold and treasures he was looking for?

Royal Welcome

Columbus spent the next few months going from island to island searching for the mainland of India, with all its riches. On Christmas Eve, 1492, he was out on the *Santa Maria* when a coral reef shattered his ship. Fortunately, a fleet of canoes led by a local king, *Guakanagaree* (GWA-kahn-ah-gah-REE), raced to help him. The dignified king and his men saved Columbus's valuables. Then, the king invited everyone to a "barbecue" that evening.

"Barbecue": Not an Oop-Word

The words "barbecue" and also "hammock" may be out of place in the English language, but they certainly are *not* out of place in America! Both words come from the *Arawak* language, spoken by the Taino of America.

"Barbecue" was the native word for bread baked outside on heated rocks. As for hammocks, if you have ever lain in one, you know how great they can be!

Try It!

Try baking bread the Taino way on a hot rock during the hottest part of a hot day. First scrub and dry a large flat rock. Set the rock to heat up in the hot sun.

Mix ¼ cup (50 ml) of Bisquick (or cornbread mix) and a tablespoon (15 ml) of water. It will make a thick dough. Put a little lump of dough on the rock and let it bake in the sun.

THINK about it!

What Is True Wealth?

The wise and capable king that Columbus met worked alongside his people. His life was not a luxurious one, but he and his people had everything they needed to be happy. On the other hand, Columbus seemed to want riches and fame; a lot of people still want those same things.

What is wealth? Is it living in a mansion, wearing expensive clothes, and owning every video game there is? Or is there more to wealth than that? Here are some questions to help you get started exploring the idea of wealth.

$ When you make a wish, what do you usually wish for?

$ Do you think rich people are happier than others?

$ What is most important to you? (Name three things.)

$ If you could be very rich, but had no family or friends, would you be happy?

$ What if you had plenty of money, but were too sick to enjoy it?

$ Is there something, aside from money, that would make you *feel* rich?

One Event: Two Points of View

A point of view is one way of looking at a situation. There are as many points of view as there are people. Often, people experience the very same event in very different ways.

When Columbus met the Taino king, both men were excited, but for very different reasons. Columbus thought he was in the Indies, close to finding a lot of gold. The king thought he was meeting a new and exotic trading partner.

Columbus gave the Taino king a red cape, and the king gave Columbus a golden belt. The king's gift was a gesture of friendship, meaning "Let's trade." But to Columbus, the gift meant that the Taino king was giving away his kingdom!

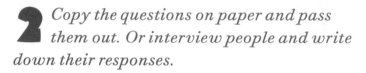

TAKE A SURVEY

What do others in your family, school, or neighborhood think about wealth?

1 *Create a survey using the questions on page 83 and others of your own.*

2 *Copy the questions on paper and pass them out. Or interview people and write down their responses.*

3 *Count and organize the answers, putting the numbers into percentages. For example, if 7 out of 10 people say "yes" to a certain question, then your results would be that 70 percent of the people surveyed believe that question is true.*

4 *On a clean sheet of paper, write or graph the results. Are you surprised by the results?*

Trouble In Paradise

When Columbus left the Taino island that he named *Hispaniola* (his-pan-NYO-la) to go back to Spain, he is said to have left with a nasty parting gesture: He bombed the remains of the *Santa Maria* to bits! That night, he wrote in his journal, "I want the natives to fear me." Nine months later, he returned with 17 ships and hundreds of men. This time he had come for the gold, and he would do *anything* for it!

Using dogs, swords, and guns, the Spaniards enslaved the Taino as they would later enslave the Mayan, Aztec, and Incan people, and some North Americans, too. The Taino had to dig for gold all day long and serve the Spaniards at night. If they did not find gold — which actually wasn't very plentiful — the Spaniards might cut off their hands.

Under this cruelty, the Taino began to die. Some became ill with diseases brought by the Europeans. Others jumped off cliffs rather than live as slaves.

Within 50 years of Columbus's arrival, the Taino people were officially declared extinct. But officials and experts can sometimes be wrong. Thank goodness that some Taino people still exist!

Internet Discovery: Meet the Taino of Today!

The descendants of the Taino who survived are part of our world today. Meet them on the World Wide Web at the Taino Cultural Interest Group at <**http://hometown.aol.com/STaino/intro.html**>.

The site has pictures of ancient artifacts, modern-day art, and poems by living Taino. They like to hear from kids, too!

Tragedy in the Indies and an Uneasy Grave

Failing to find much gold, Columbus decided to make money by *selling* the Taino as slaves in Spain.

When Queen Isabella found out, she flew into a rage and made him stop. Slavery did stop, but only in Spain. It continued in the West Indies, far from Isabella's view. When the Taino died from overwork, Africans were brought in to replace them.

Columbus made three more trips back and forth across the Atlantic, but he never found the gold and riches that he hoped for.

In 1506, at the age of 54, he died in Spain, still certain that he had discovered a new route to the Indies.

But Everyone Else Says (Knows, Does...!)

All cultures share beliefs and ideas. When the beliefs are positive, that can be wonderful. For instance, most people who live in the United States — no matter what their cultural heritage — believe that it's important to be free.

But cultures can share ignorant, destructive, or dangerous beliefs, too. Some people think their cultures are better than others, for instance. They haven't learned that "different" does not mean better or worse. And mistreatment of the natives and others didn't start or stop with Columbus.

In those situations, the voices of brave individuals are needed more than ever to speak up for justice!

The Final Mystery

HERE LIES
CHRISTOPHER
COLUMBUS
(WE THINK)

Here's an odd twist to the Columbus story: No one is sure where Columbus is buried! Thirty-four years after Columbus's death, Diego's wife asked that Christopher's remains be shipped to Hispaniola, where Diego was buried.

However, in 1795, France conquered Hispaniola, and the remains were moved to Cuba. Then, in 1898, they were sent from Cuba to Spain! A casket with Columbus's name still exists in Spain.

While the admiral's bones were supposedly resting in Spain, however, a second casket with his name was found on Hispaniola. No one is certain which casket has the real remains, and neither country wants to find out! (The remains are tourist attractions in both places. Now, Columbus would have liked that!)

One writer said of Columbus, "It is as difficult to pin down the location of his bones as it is to pin down his place in history."

When the Truth Changes

What happens when something we've learned proves to be untrue? For example, if you were taught that Columbus was a good and brave man, is it upsetting to you to find that he was also cruel?

When our ideas about the truth change, we may feel that we have been lied to, though that is rarely the case. Most inaccurate ideas and information are passed along to us with good, honest intentions.

Or we may feel foolish, as though we have missed out on knowing the truth all along. That can make us wonder what else we "know" that isn't totally accurate.

But the wondering is actually a very good thing, because it leads us to all sorts of new discoveries. By updating our ideas, adding new information, and replacing inaccurate beliefs, we can only become smarter and, sometimes, even wiser.

It seems there is a lot of changing scenery on the road to truth. Instead of getting upset by the changes, it's probably best to learn to enjoy them and keep moving forward.

Columbus's Twenty-First Century Report Card

If Columbus were a student judged by today's standards, he might get a report card with comments like these:

Report Card

Language	B+	Columbus's ship's log (journal) was very well written.
Science	A+	Columbus surmised that planet Earth was round and that by traveling west he could reach the East.
Geography	D	Columbus *insisted* that he had found India and that Cuba was Japan!
Math	C	Despite good effort, Columbus made many mistakes measuring land and water distances.
Bravery	A	Columbus faced his fears and went where no one else had gone before.
Determination	A	Columbus worked hard and faced obstacles for years in order to make his dream come true.
Leadership	F	Columbus could not control his crew or those he governed, particularly when he was governor of Hispaniola.
Treating Others with Respect	F-	Columbus treated the native people of America horribly and made no effort to understand or appreciate their way of life.

WHAT ABOUT COLUMBUS DAY?

With all you have heard about Columbus, do you still believe in celebrating Columbus Day? Or would you rather replace it with another holiday?

1 *In Australia, where natives suffered mistreatment in the past, people observe Sorry Day to help heal the wounds of the past. Australians come together on that day to learn about the aborigines (native peoples of Australia) and to help them preserve their traditional way of life.*

2 *Make a new American holiday to celebrate the Americas and replace Columbus Day. What would your holiday honor, and what would you name it? How would you celebrate it?*

Take the "Star Guide" Challenge!

Where do Christopher Columbus's escapades fall on your *Star Guide?*

Just the Beginning

The impact of Columbus and the Spanish explorers who followed was just the beginning of events that would change America forever.

The rest, as they say, is history!

Adding It All Up!

Congratulations! You have just completed your own discovery. Your exploration went all the way from the Land-Bridge Theory to Columbus's ocean voyage.

You've investigated and tested theories and ideas, you've tracked truth, followed clues, sorted through evidence, and tuned into your own hunches. Your accomplishment has been to "descry" (see page 11) the discovery of America. From far away in time, you've examined, thought, and felt your way through the mystery to get closer to what makes the most sense to you. *So, take a bow for all the discoveries that you've made!*

And now here you are at the end of a book, but at the *beginning* of a deeper understanding of what discovery and America are really all about.

So, Who *Really* Discovered America?

O kay, Truth Tracker, it's time to settle up. Throughout this book, you have investigated all sorts of theories about America's original discovery. How do they all stack up in *your* opinion?

Use the *Star Guide* on page 22 to decide if one theory over all others makes most sense. If it does, give that theory a number to represent how close or far you believe it is from the truth. Let 25 stand for totally true and 0 stand for completely false.

Which of these theories comes closest to the truth and earns your highest score?

The Land-Bridge Theory (pages 23–24)	The African-Influence Theory (pages 59–60)
The Multiple-Migration Theory (page 32)	The Asian Theory (page 61)
The Woden-lithi Theory (pages 33–34)	The Other-Way-Around Theory (pages 62–63)
The Native Theory (pages 39–40)	The Vikings' Adventure (pages 64–74)
The Alien Theory (pages 43–46)	Columbus's Adventure (pages 75–89)

The conclusion you draw will be your best idea for now. But remember, new information is always being uncovered, and the question will remain open in the future!

Discovery Never Ends

After Columbus, many others came to "discover" America. Some were merchants, like Henry Hudson, who "discovered" a harbor and created the city of New Amsterdam, which later became New York City. Some were conquerors like Pizarro and Cortés, who took over whole societies in South America.

Over hundreds of years, people kept coming in the hope of finding freedom and good fortune in America. Waves of immigrants came, families came, individuals came. All of them discovered America for themselves — and they are still coming today, adding to the rich experience that we call America.

For those of us who are already here, the discovery continues. Every time you get curious, or open your mind, or think something through — every time you decide to use your energy to make a better world or be a better son, daughter, or friend — a new and better America is being discovered — *by you!*

INDEX

MORE GOOD BOOKS FROM
WILLIAMSON PUBLISHING

Kaleidoscope Kids® books, for kids ages 7–14, explore a single subject in depth from many perspectives, using many different thinking skills and hands-on activities. All books are 96 pages, two-color, fully illustrated, 10 x 10, $10.95 US.

American Bookseller Pick of the Lists
Children's Book Council Notable Book
Dr. Toy 10 Best Educational Products
PYRAMIDS!
50 Hands-On Activities to Experience Ancient Egypt
by Avery Hart & Paul Mantell

American Bookseller Pick of the Lists
Parents' Guide Children's Media Award
ANCIENT GREECE!
40 Hands-On Activities to Experience This Wondrous Age
by Avery Hart & Paul Mantell

American Bookseller Pick of the Lists
Children's Book Council Notable Book
Dr. Toy 100 Best Children's Products
KNIGHTS & CASTLES
50 Hands-On Activities to Experience the Middle Ages
by Avery Hart & Paul Mantell

GOING WEST!
Journey on a Wagon Train to Settle a Frontier Town
by Carol A. Johmann and Elizabeth J. Rieth

American Bookseller Pick of the Lists
¡MEXICO!
40 Activities to Experience Mexico Past and Present
by Susan Milord

Parents' Choice Recommended
BRIDGES!
Amazing Structures to Design, Build & Test
by Carol A. Johmann and Elizabeth J. Rieth

SKYSCRAPERS!
Amazing Structures to Design & Build
by Carol A. Johmann

Teachers' Choice Award
GEOLOGY ROCKS!
50 Hands-On Activities to Explore the Earth
by Cindy Blobaum

THE BEAST IN YOU!
Activities & Questions to Explore Evolution
by Marc McCutcheon

Prices may be slightly higher when purchased in Canada.

To see what's new at Williamson and learn more about specific books, visit our website at:
www.williamsonbooks.com

To Order Williamson Books:

We accept Visa and MasterCard.
(Please include the number and expiration date.)

Toll-free phone orders with credit cards:
1-800-234-8791

Or, send a check with your order to:
Williamson Publishing Company
P.O. Box 185
Charlotte, Vermont 05445

Please add $4.00 for postage for one book plus $1.00 for each additional book.
Satisfaction is guaranteed or full refund without questions or quibbles.